DATE DUE

THE
FRENCH RIVIERA
CAMPAIGN

of August 1944

ALAN F. WILT

Southern Illinois University Press

Copyright © 1981 by Southern Illinois University Press
All rights reserved
Printed in the United States of America
Edited by Stephen W. Smith
Designed by Guy Fleming
Production supervised by Richard Neal

Library of Congress Cataloging in Publication Data

Wilt, Alan F
The French Riviera Campaign of August 1944.

Bibliography: p.
Includes index.
1. World War, 1939-1945—Campaigns—France—Riviera.
2. Riviera—History.   I. Title.
D762.R5W54   940.54'21   80-23041
ISBN 0–8093–1000–7

CONTENTS

Illustrations and Maps

Vice Adm. H. Kent Hewitt talking with a beachmaster
French Tabors begin moving toward the front lines
United States 45th Division soldiers move ahead
An American soldier walks past a picture of the Fuehrer
French Resistance fighters deal with a collaborator
Wounded being carried along the beach
French victory parade in Toulon
French troops engaged in house-to-house fighting in Marseilles
Effects of German harbor demolitions in Marseilles
"Big Willie" guns
An American tank rolls past destroyed German vehicles
Allied soldiers and French partisans cleaning out German snipers
American infantrymen moving out on a tank
Members of the 3rd Division crossing the Doubs River
A French girl gives a bottle of wine to T.Sgt. Joe Tradenick
Lieutenant General Devers with French Generals de Lattre, Béthouart, and Monsabert

MAPS

PREFACE

It is surprising that no author has written a full-length study of the French Riviera campaign, for the landing of August 15, 1944, brings together a number of interesting features: a spirited exchange between British and American leaders, an amphibious invasion of considerable proportions, a swift Allied advance led by colorful, yet competent commanders. Nevertheless, little has been published on the invasion of southern France. There is no official history on the subject to date, and the naval and air official histories cover only portions of the topic. The only complete treatment, Jacques Robichon's *Le debarquement de Provence* (English edition: *The Second D-Day*) is not a critical, balanced account. Pierre Guiral's *Libération de Marseille* does not focus primarily on the invasion, and Marshal Jean de Lattre de Tassigny's *The History of the First French Army* concentrates on France's role in the campaign. British works, such as John Ehrman's Volume 5 in the *Grand Strategy* series and Sir Stephen Roskill's third volume of his monumental *The War at Sea, 1939–1945*, deal only with Britain's role. Maurice Matloff's essay in Kent Roberts Greenfield's *Command Decisions*, Robert H. Adelman's and George Walton's popularized *The Champagne Campaign*, and Jörg Staiger's *Rückzug durchs Rhônetal* likewise examine only portions of the operation. My book is therefore the first attempt to present a balanced treatment of the French Riviera campaign as well as to make the invasion better appreciated and understood.

A number of individuals were kind enough to assist me in preparing this volume. Robin Higham took time out of his incredibly busy schedule to read and comment on the entire manuscript. Colleagues John Dobson and Alston J. Shakeshaft also made numerous suggestions and criticisms which greatly improved the writing style and added to my understanding of the campaign. Gen. Theodore Conway, Forrest

Pogue, and Dean Allard graciously shared with me their knowledge on specific points.

I owe an equally large debt of gratitide to the scores of archivists who went out of their way to help me in my research endeavors. Among them were Robert Wolfe, George Wagner, and especially William Cunliffe of the United States National Archives; Dean Allard of the Naval History Division in Washington; Hannah Zeidlik of the Center of Military History; B. Franklin Cooling and Richard Sommers of the United States Army Military History Research Collection, Carlisle Barracks, Pennsylvania; and Landon Reisinger of the York County Historical Society, York, Pennsylvania. Col. Thomas Griess granted me permission to use the papers of Gen. Jacob L. Devers, located at York. I should also like to express my appreciation to the staffs of the Library of Congress; the Washington National Records Center, Suitland, Maryland; the Public Records Office and the British Library in London; and the Bundesarchiv-Militärarchiv in Freiburg i. Br. for their courteous assistance. Photographs were provided by courtesy of the United States Army, the United States Air Force, and the United States National Archives.

Equally great is my obligation to Iowa State's University Research Foundation and to the University's Sciences and Humanities Research Institute which granted me time and money to pursue the project at critical junctures. Laurie Helmers cheerfully typed and retyped the manuscript, and James Simmons and Stephen Smith of Southern Illinois University Press were very helpful in the final editing of the book. Errors which remain are, of course, my responsibility. Above all, I wish to express my thanks publicly to my wife, Maureen, for her steadying influence and unfailing encouragement.

Alan F. Wilt

Ames, Iowa
September 1980

THE

FRENCH RIVIERA

CAMPAIGN

of August 1944

1

The Anvil Debate

O N AUGUST 15 1944, American and French amphibious forces began an invasion of southern France. Surprisingly, its overwhelming success has not evoked the acclaim and interest given other, often less successful, Allied campaigns. The reason seems to be tied in with the circumstances surrounding the planning and execution of Anvil, as the operation was called. For behind the victory lay a serious divergence of opinion, a controversy between American and British leaders which tended, if not to disrupt, at least to warp Anglo-American wartime relations for many months preceding the assault. Both then and now, the basic cause for disagreement between the two sides was simply this question: Was the invasion really necessary?

The British definitely felt it was not. Almost from the time the Americans first proposed Anvil at the Quebec Conference in August 1943, Churchill was opposed to it, and he consistently tried to block its implementation. During late 1943 and into 1944, the great wartime Prime Minister and his Chiefs of Staff contended that the buildup for Overlord must be accorded top priority, although they agreed that exigencies on the Italian front and the strategic bombing offensive also had to be taken into account. By January 1944, British and American leaders feared, however, that the Normandy invasion might be held up because of a lack of landing craft. Since the Mediterranean theater was an important source for this precious commodity, Anvil, even though it was to complement Overlord and to take place simultaneously with it, had to be postponed in deference to the cross-Channel attack.

After June 6, Churchill was determined that any new, major effort in the Mediterranean should assist Field Marshal Sir Harold Alexander in his Italian campaign rather than squandering forces needlessly on a diversion into southern France. But Churchill did not succeed in sidetracking the operation, and on July 2, the Allies agreed that Anvil (now changed to Dragoon as a security precaution) should proceed on August 15. Still he did not give up. At the end of July he came up with a scheme to switch the amphibious assault from the French Riviera coast to the Brittany peninsula so that the Allies could better exploit the United States breakout of the Normandy beachhead near Saint-Lô. The Americans once again resisted Churchill's last attempt, but by the time it was resolved only one week remained before Dragoon was to be executed. In other words, its implementation took place in spite of his many machinations against it.

The Americans' view of the French Riviera campaign was decidedly different. President Roosevelt and his military advisors never wavered in their desire to undertake Anvil/Dragoon in conjunction with the Normandy operation, since they always considered it an essential concomitant to assure Overlord's success. They thought that the British also favored a cross-Channel invasion, but believed that their "closest" ally, under the guise of flexibility, wanted additional operations in the Mediterranean, including a major campaign in the Balkans. To the Americans, such a course of action only courted disaster. It would violate the military principle of concentration of force, would help fritter away the initiative in the west, and would place American combat soldiers in an area in which the United States had little interest.

On the other hand, they believed that a campaign aimed at the French Riviera held out the prospect of substantial benefits. It would engage large numbers of Axis troops, not as many as before June 6, but still a force of considerable size. It would release immediately numerous French formations for combat on French soil. It would open up the possibility of capturing major ports, thereby contributing greatly to the Allied supply effort. And, finally, it would increase the pressure even more on Germany from the west. Even after Overlord had succeeded, the Americans still considered Dragoon to be a vital element in their overall strategy.

Though somewhat overshadowed by the prior United States-British controversy, the conduct of the campaign itself must also be taken into account in any attempt to determine whether the invasion should ever have taken place. The assault along the French Riviera, followed by the rapid, 400-mile advance to the Belfort Gap in eastern France, made it appear as almost a model operation. To be sure, its phenomenal success does not alone tip the scale conclusively in favor of those who advocated the operation, since one might contend that its very success shows that the invasion was unnecessary. But obviously it is an important factor and must be considered in any assessment of the Anvil/Dragoon undertaking.

Another point which must be borne in mind, and one alluded to earlier, is that Anvil was never conceived as an operation in its own right. It was always considered subsidiary to the Normandy campaign and other operations that were being planned and executed during the course of 1944.

As a consequence, it never received the backing, much less the subsequent notoriety, of Overlord or the 1944 Russian offensive or even the campaign in Italy.

Nevertheless, the Provençal invasion is a very significant and comprehensive campaign. It is interesting to chart the strategic talks and memoranda exchanged between Churchill and Roosevelt, the discussions—at times heated—among their headstrong and intelligent military advisors, and the vital, detailed planning undertaken by experienced staff officers in the Mediterranean theater. At the same time, it is important to note the German thinking and defensive preparations, for the deteriorating situation in southern France, especially after the Normandy invasion, goes a long way toward explaining the ease of the Allied success. Finally, the actual invasion brings together a number of features: a combined operation of considerable magnitude which utilized land, air, and naval forces, airborne and commando units, and battle-hardened assault troops; an ordered and on the whole orderly German withdrawal; several daring attacks by French forces to capture the ports of Toulon and Marseilles; and a colorful yet competent group of American and French commanders who led the soldiers in their swift, northerly advance. In short, the French Riviera operation contains all of the elements which eventually combined to bring about the Allied victory in the Second World War.

By August 1943, the Allies had assumed the offensive everywhere and had achieved notable victories on a number of fronts. Sicily had been invaded and success assured. The Soviets had blunted the long-awaited German operation at Kursk and had started their own offensives in central and southern Russia. The long American trek across the Pacific toward Japan was also underway. In the air, the Combined Bomber Offensive was starting to show results. Even more importantly, the battle of the Atlantic had been won, thus assuring that the invasion of western Europe would eventually become a reality. The Allies now set about to translate their hard-found victories into a common, winning strategy.

With growing confidence, American and British leaders gathered in Quebec to continue their series of conferences, which had begun even before the United States formally entered the war in December 1941. At Quadrant, as the August 14–23 meeting was called, Churchill and Roosevelt and their advisors dealt with a number of important issues. Most immediately, they confirmed that Italy was to be next and that secret peace negotiations with the new Italian government be set in motion at once. In addition, they reaffirmed and scheduled Overlord for the spring of 1944 and approved plans for stepped-up operations in the Pacific and in northern Burma.

A number of other matters were also discussed, though they did not require a firm decision. Among them, the American Joint Chiefs of Staff presented a memorandum proposing an amphibious landing in southern France. The objective of the operation, as they conceived it, was to secure a lodgment in the Marseilles area and thereby "assist Overlord by containing maximum German forces."[1] The memorandum envisaged that, exclusive of ten divisions deemed essential to maintain pressure against the enemy in northern Italy, ten United States and British and four French divisions plus sufficient air and naval support were to be allocated for the initial two-division lift. The beachhead was then to be secured by "strong reinforcements, overland if feasible from northern Italy, and by sea within the limits of available shipping."

The British did not object to the American proposal at the time. The only modifications they asked for and received were that, in addition to establishing a lodgment in the Toulon-Marseilles area, Allied troops should be prepared to move northward, and that the operation should not be restricted solely to forces available in the Mediterranean theater. Britain's apparently agreeable attitude is not difficult to understand. The American suggestion was highly speculative (the Italian mainland had not yet even been invaded); it did not commit the British to anything; and it tied in well with their main objective at the conference, namely, to get the Americans to realize that operations in the Mediterranean and the proposed Normandy campaign were complementary and closely linked. United States military leaders were also well satisfied at the end of the meeting. Not only had the British accepted the idea of a landing in southern France. They had also reaffirmed their commitment to Overlord, a commitment on which the Americans had been fearful the British were backsliding in favor of a Balkan operation.

At the conclusion of the conference, the United States and British Combined Chiefs directed General Eisenhower, then serving as the Supreme Allied Commander in the Mediterranean, to submit an outline plan for a possible operation in southern France. Eisenhower's response toward the end of October was less than enthusiastic.[2] He pointed out that because of a lack of landing craft in the theater, no more than one division could be used in the initial assault, and that the subsequent buildup would be greatly hampered unless a large port were taken quickly and made operational. Moreover, he stated, "it would be strategically unsound" to decide now that Anvil was definitely the best contribution this theater could make in support of Overlord. Reflecting the British view, the American commander went even further. "The South of France," he said, "cannot be logically considered by itself." One must consider the Mediterranean as a whole. "Operations in Italy, carefully timed to correspond with Overlord, may prove more valuable than a necessarily iso-

lated and small-scale operation against Southern France."
Surprisingly, British Lt. Gen. Sir Frederick Morgan, the top
planner for Overlord, did not agree with Eisenhower.[3] He
felt that the *only* possible way to tie down German forces in
the south of France was to undertake Anvil simultaneously
with the cross-Channel attack. Morgan's view made it clear
that the United States and Great Britain had no settled policy
with regard to southern France.

The issue remained unsettled when the main Allied
heads of state met at Cairo and Tehran in late November and
early December of 1943. Although areas of disagreement
among the major partners were in evidence during the conferences, these meetings still probably represent the high
point of Allied cooperation during the war. It was obvious
that the war had turned in their favor. To be sure, the campaign in Italy had bogged down, but British and United
States leaders could point to other substantial victories since
mid-1943 that more than offset this disappointment—the
rapid takeover of Sicily, the opening up of the Atlantic, the
increasingly effective, if costly, Combined Bomber Offensive.
The Soviets were also in a favorable frame of mind. Their
advances on the central and southern fronts had yielded impressive gains, and supplies from the West were finally beginning to make an impact.

In this heady atmosphere, a number of the outstanding
military issues were resolved. Overlord, Stalin's long-awaited
second front, was accorded top priority and reaffirmed as
taking place sometime the following May. Continuing American fears of a British adventure in the Balkans or the eastern
Mediterranean were quieted—at least for the moment. In
support of Overlord, the Soviets promised an all-out offensive on the eastern front. And to assure the success of the
Normandy campaign, Buccaneer, an amphibious assault
against the Andaman Islands off the Burmese coast, was to

be abandoned (much to Chiang Kai-shek's displeasure) because of a lack of landing craft.

The fate of the operation in southern France was also decided, but in a rather curious way. In their first formal meeting, Roosevelt, Churchill, and Stalin were ruminating about possible operations in the Mediterranean. At one point in the discussion the Soviet dictator declared that he thought it would be a mistake to disperse forces in the area. As he saw it: "The best course would be to make Overlord the basic operation for 1944, and once Rome had been captured, to send all available forces in Italy to Southern France. These forces could then join hands with the Overlord forces when the invasion was launched. France was the weakest spot on the German front."[4] Although Roosevelt's response to Stalin was direct and favorable, both he and Churchill were surprised at Stalin's sudden interest in southern France. In fact, as the official British historian has pointed out, they had not even brought Eisenhower's October outline plan with them.[5] The only paper they had available was the original American proposal presented in August and now long out of date.

Stalin and his chief military advisor, Marshal Voroshilov, went on to reiterate their suggestion at several subsequent sessions. In a meeting with his American and British counterparts, Voroshilov, who saw the war in the west in typical Soviet tactical and strategic fashion, put the military position succinctly: "Italy offered great possibilities for defense. Defense could be organized there with a minimum of troops. The remaining troops could be used for the South of France in order to attack the enemy from two sides." While disputing Voroshilov's idea of a great pincer movement (Normandy and France's Mediterranean coast were more than 500 miles apart), the United States and British Chiefs of Staff could also see great merit in a southern France invasion. In the end they recommended to Roosevelt and Churchill that the latter "inform Marshal Stalin that we will launch Overlord in May, in conjunction with a supporting operation against the South of France on the largest scale that is permitted by landing craft available at the time." The two leaders accepted the recommendation. Anvil had now become an integral part of Allied strategy.

The Tehran decision on Anvil was indeed an important one. The United States and Britain had resolved—with a push from Russia—that an invasion of southern France, in support of Overlord, was to take place. One might contend, as a number of subsequent writers have done, that the Soviets were actually more interested in deflecting the West from operations in the Balkans or Turkey than they were in a southern France landing. But this does not seem to be the case. The Soviets—at least at this point, the end of 1943— were obsessed with the idea of a second front. They sincerely believed, though they did not insist, that Anvil was the best way to support it from the Mediterranean.

Also resolved was the issue of timing. A good deal of discussion had occurred both at Cairo and at Tehran as to whether Anvil should be scheduled before, during, or after the Normandy landing. Now it had been decided: Anvil and Overlord were to take place at the same time. Finally, the agreement recognized that a lack of landing craft could well determine the size, if not jeopardize the very existence, of the operation.

While the issues had been examined and for the most part resolved, a number of other problems still remained. They were turned over, as a matter of urgency, to Eisenhower's staff in Algiers. This time the planners were given more guidance and latitude than earlier in the year. They were to presume that the landing in southern France would take place sometime in May. They were to assume that Allied forces at the time had reached and were holding the Pisa-

Florence-Rimini line across central Italy. They were to be given enough shipping and assault craft for an initial lift of at least two divisions. And to assure sufficient men and material, they were to submit a list of resources which could not be made available in the Mediterranean area.

A number of other events which had occurred during the fall of 1943 also lightened Eisenhower's task. The Italian peninsula had proved difficult to penetrate, but Italy had been defeated, had left the Axis side, and had joined the Allies as a cobelligerent in November. Enough of Italy had been occupied to establish a strategic air force, the United States Fifteenth, in the area. While its primary mission was to assist bombers from the United Kingdom in the offensive against Germany, it could also be used, of course, for urgent tasks in the Mediterranean. Most importantly, and directly related to Anvil, Free French forces with the help of Resistance fighters had liberated Corsica in September and early October, and the island was already being transformed into a staging area and base for air operations against the southern French coast.

Eisenhower's detailed plan was ready by Christman Eve.[6] To a large degree, it reflected the guidelines set forth at Tehran and Cairo: a two- or three-division assault, building up eventually to ten divisions; a May target date; a holding operation in Italy. But planners also added a number of new features. The total force was to consist of three or four American divisions, and the rest were to be French, since the French were being organized and equipped in North Africa along United States lines. It was to be made up of eight infantry and two armored divisions with battle-trained regimental combat teams (meaning American) leading the initial assault. The plan also called for airborne formations and commando units to secure the flanks and prevent enemy reinforcements from reaching the beachhead. The navy's convoy and fire support requirements were to be met primarily from resources in the area, as were those of the air forces, with the exception that the air contribution might be augmented with carrier-borne aircraft. As for the French resistance forces, any help received from them would be looked upon as a bonus.

To the when—in May—was added the where. Eisenhower's appreciation gave a detailed appraisal of the possibilities along France's 400-mile, Mediterranean coastline and concluded that there were only two logical possibilities. One of them, near Sète in the west, was ruled out as having too small a harbor capacity—and the quick capture of a port was thought to be essential. It would also be outside the range of Corsica-based fighter aircraft. The other possibility, east of Toulon, was considered more attractive. It was near the large port of Marseilles (Toulon, though of great psychological value as the home of the French fleet, was thought to be sufficient only temporarily for supply purposes). The beaches were big enough for a large followup force, and the terrain suitable for the rapid construction of airstrips. With these criteria in mind, it was concluded that the Rade d'Hyères beaches, fifteen to twenty miles east of Toulon, best met these requirements. But "should the defense of the Rade prove to be so strong as to make assault there too hazardous, the Cavalaire–Cap Camarat area [a little farther east] would serve as an alternative."

The operation itself, which took into account the previous amphibious experiences in North Africa, Sicily, and Italy, was to take place in four phases. The preliminary phase, which was already in being, was to consist of unspecified measures to weaken German resistance in the area. At D day minus 42 concerted air action was to begin, eventually reaching its climax at the time of the attack. Phase three was to be made up of the all-important assault phase and capture

Southern France with German Troop Dispositions

of a port. The plan envisaged French troops taking Toulon by D + 5, but German forces in Marseilles, the main prize forty miles west of Toulon, were expected to hold out for some time. Only after Marseilles was in Allied hands and the beachhead secured, was the final phase, a push north aimed at the Lyons and Vichy areas, to be undertaken.

By the end of 1943, then, most of the essential requirements had been worked out, but without sacrificing flexibility. Anvil was to consist of United States and French land forces with the British—busy in Italy—assuming virtually no role, except in the vital areas of naval and air support. The place, the Rade d'Hyères, had been selected, but with another alternative still under consideration. And, just as important, planners now had a much better idea of the problems involved in launching an invasion against southern France. The command structure, however, was far from settled. General Eisenhower had been named supreme commander for Overlord, and he quite naturally desired to take a number of his staff officers and field commanders with him. Lt. Gen. George S. Patton, Jr., already well known for his armored exploits, would seem to have been the logical choice to handle the detailed planning in the Mediterranean as head of Seventh Army. But he had become involved in several "slapping incidents" of soldiers and had to be relieved of his command. These measures dictated wholesale command changes in the Mediterranean theater.

After some haggling between British and American leaders it was decided that the new overall Mediterranean commander would be British. Their Chiefs of Staff ultimately concluded that Field Marshal Sir Maitland Wilson, nicknamed "Jumbo" for his girth, was not too old and could fill Eisenhower's former position. Jacob L. Devers, the most senior American general in Britain, was shifted to the Mediterranean to serve as Wilson's deputy.

A native of York, Pennsylvania, and West Pointer, Devers had gotten along well with his British counterparts while stationed in England and was expected to do the same in the Mediterranean theater. Churchill had originally wanted Eisenhower's deputy, Brig. Gen. W. Bedell Smith, for the post, but the Prime Minister did not push the point since Ike was unwilling to give up his chief of staff.

Happily, the choice of Devers was a good one for the Americans. His familiarity with the British had not led to what was called "localitis," or undue preference for the British point of view, and he steadfastly supported the position of the United States Joint Chiefs, and especially that of General Marshall, the army chief of staff, with regard to Anvil. Though he had long been in Marshall's confidence, the latter's letter to Devers on December 28, 1943, was terse and to the point. "You will probably be assigned as the American commander in the Mediterranean theater under Wilson and as his Deputy Commander. Your experience in dealing with the British and other Allied Headquarters qualifies you for this assignment."[7] Devers was not particularly overjoyed with the change, for he longed for a combat command, a position he had never held. But he accepted the new assignment with good grace, especially since his only other prospect was to remain in England, where his future was uncertain.

At the same time, Lt. Gen. Ira C. Eaker, the commander of the United States strategic Eighth Air Force in England, was named to head the Mediterranean Allied Air Forces, replacing Air Chief Marshal Sir Arthur Tedder, Ike's deputy in North Africa and Sicily, who was to fulfill a similar position as deputy commander for Overlord. The changes were further complicated by the fact that Eaker now needed a British deputy. Air Marshal Sir John Slessor, a highly regarded and experienced commander then stationed in England, was named to the post. To replace Eaker, Ike's choice fell on his former top American air commander in the Mediterranean, Lt. Gen. Carl A. "Tooey" Spaatz. Like Devers, the balding Eaker did not look upon the switch with great favor, especially since air attacks from England were now beginning to reach their stride. But in February he did admit to Air Chief Marshal Sir Arthur Harris, the head of British Bomber Command, with regard to his new job, that "there is much to do and it has some interesting aspects."[8]

As for the navy, it would remain under the overall direction of Adm. Sir John Cunningham. While he was not related to the more famous admiral, Sir Andrew Cunningham, who became First Sea Lord in late 1943, Sir John was an experienced Mediterranean commander in his own right and a very able officer. Another highly regarded commander, United States Adm. H. Kent Hewitt, head of the Eighth Fleet, was to direct the projected Anvil task force.

Moreover, the problem of filling the Seventh Army command position was also thought to be solved. Gen. Mark Clark, then commanding the Fifth Army in Italy, was eventually to give up that position in order to direct the operation in southern France. For the time being, he was temporarily placed in charge of both Fifth and Seventh armies. To lead the assault phase, Clark wanted Gen. Lucian K. Truscott, one of his corps commanders, although he had to ward off the entreaties of Eisenhower, who also wanted Truscott, "because he is the finest combat commander in the corps and divisional levels we now have on the front."[9]

Nevertheless, the command structure was now for the most part set. Field Marshal Wilson, a veteran of numerous Mediterranean campaigns, was to serve as theater commander with General Eaker, Admiral Cunningham, and General Clark directing the overall land, sea, and air phases.

The actual assault forces were to be under Admiral Hewitt and General Truscott; only the tactical air commander had not yet been picked.

Therefore, several of the stumbling blocks which might have prevented Anvil from being executed had been removed. But almost from the time Eisenhower's plan had been accepted toward the end of December, a series of events began to take place that threatened the very existence of the operation. General Morgan, the chief Overlord planner, who had favored Anvil in its earlier, weakened form, was alarmed that it had become an operation of such major proportions. Overlord, he pointed out on January 8, was conceived on a narrow margin and could succeed more readily if broadened to a four- or five- rather than a three-division assault front as now planned.[10] He felt that the southern France attack should revert to a one-division threat, and that additional resources, especially landing craft, should be reallocated to strengthen Overlord. The renowned Gen. Sir Bernard Montgomery, who was to command all Allied ground forces during the landing phase of Overlord, also questioned the soundness of mounting the Normandy operation on a three-divisional front, and even Bedell Smith agreed that it should be expanded at the expense of Anvil.[11] Thus, by the time Eisenhower, who had been on leave in the United States, arrived in London in mid-January, Anvil was already in jeopardy.

Meanwhile, Allied operations in Italy did nothing to enhance Anvil's status. A Fifth Army offensive started well on January 10 but had become bogged down before the end of the month. An amphibious assault at Anzio south of Rome was launched on January 22, but it, too, stalled in the face of stiffening German resistance. Therefore, by the beginning of February, Anvil had clearly become buffeted between the requirements of Overlord on the one hand and the worsening situation in Italy on the other.

At this point the Anvil debate began in earnest. The United States Joint Chiefs in a memorandum on January 31 rejected the notion of a one-division threat and put forth every argument they could think of in support of an operation in southern France.[12] It was the best way to make effective use of French and American forces now in the Mediterranean. It was essential to the success of Overlord. It had been agreed to at Tehran, the implication being that the Soviet Union had also agreed to it. The memorandum even went so far as to declare, "Our examination shows that there is now allocated to the Mediterranean sufficient assault shipping and craft to mount at least a two-division assault for Anvil, and that it might even be as large as 2-⅔ divisions." The Joint Chiefs did make one concession, however. They felt that Overlord might be *"closely followed* by a satisfactory supporting operation against the south of France," rather than being simultaneous with it.

The reply of the British Chiefs of Staff on February 4 constituted almost a point-by-point refutation of the American position.[13] It began by stating that since a five-divisional assault front for Overlord had now become an accepted fact, only one division would be left over in the Mediterranean for Anvil. Indicating the extent to which British opposition had deepened, the memorandum continued, "Even if resources could be found to increase this lift to two divisions, we are not convinced that the most profitable use of this force would be against the South of France." In the British Chiefs' view a new factor had entered the picture. The Germans were obviously resisting the Allied advance in Italy "to the utmost of their capacity." It was therefore in the best interest of the Allies to "prosecute the Italian campaign with the utmost vigor," they argued, for it would prevent German troops from being used to reinforce France during 1944.

Then, in a point designed to show the Americans' simplistic grasp of military strategy, the memorandum continued: "It must be pointed out that the distance between Anvil and Overlord is nearly 500 miles, the country so rugged, and the defensive power of modern weapons so strong, that the pincer movement does not apply. Except as a diversionary effort, Anvil is not strategically interwoven with Overlord." As for the French, the British said they realized the disadvantages of not being able to put French forces, which were centered in the Mediterranean, into the south of France. But under the new circumstances, all Allied forces in the area would probably be needed to nourish the campaign in Italy. The British Chiefs added that serious consideration should be given to increasing French participation in the north of France. Finally, the British contended that in light of the altered situation in Italy, they did not believe that Marshal Stalin would mind where the diversionary operation took place despite the previously agreed upon diversion in southern France. The lines were clearly drawn. The United States Chiefs insisted that Anvil be carried out, though it might not be simultaneous with Overlord. The British Chiefs, as well as their senior field commanders, were equally adamant that while Overlord had top priority, developments in Italy would dictate the form that support from the Mediterranean was to take.

American support of Anvil was not, however, as united as was the British opposition. While the Joint Chiefs—Marshall, Admirals Ernest J. King and William D. Leahy, and Air Force General "Hap" Arnold—backed Anvil to a man, United States commanders in the Mediterranean were split on the issue. Devers and Admiral Hewitt favored the French Riviera operation, but Generals Clark and Eaker did not. Facing determined German opposition in Italy, Clark wanted to maintain pressure there and even suggested a possible diversionary thrust at the head of the Adriatic, a move Hewitt opposed on the grounds that it would put additional strains on the navy. Eaker had long held the position that an Adriatic thrust would make better use of existing air facilities and also opened up the prospect of erecting airfields on the Hungarian plain for the strategic air offensive against Germany. On one occasion when Eaker expressed this view to Marshall, the latter replied, "Apparently you have been with the British too long."[14]

The American Joint Chiefs, firm in their support of Anvil, were not unduly concerned about the differences of opinion in the theater. Fortunately, they also took the British criticisms in stride. Other than emphasizing once again the need for utilizing French troops in southern France, they did not seem overly upset. In this regard, Marshall undoubtedly remembered Voroshilov's statement at Tehran that "Stalin did not insist on an operation against the South of France." On February 5, he told Field Marshall Sir John Dill, the head of the British Joint Staff Mission in Washington, that he was not particularly worried about promises made to Stalin regarding Anvil, though some of his staff were anxious about it. Although not given to jocularity, he also remarked to Dill in a joking manner "that this was a great reversal of form as he found himself now trying to support Mediterranean operations and you were supporting his child."[15] In the end the Joint Chiefs decided, with British concurrence, to abide by the decision of the Supreme Allied Commander, General Eisenhower.

Ike thus found himself caught in the middle. He was intimately familiar with the plans for a strong Anvil and supported them. But, on the other hand, he was now responsible for seeing that the cross-Channel attack succeeded at all costs, even, if need be, at the price of abandoning Anvil. By February 19, with the situation in Italy stalemated and planning pressures for Overlord mounting, Eisenhower expressed his doubts about Anvil's viability and queried his American superiors about what to do. As historian Maurice Matloff relates, two days later at a special meeting in Washington, the President and his Joint Chiefs agreed that Anvil should not be canceled.[16] At about the same time, aware that Eisenhower was wavering, Field Marshal Wilson in the Mediterranean called for its cancellation. After several days of feverish negotiations between British and American military leaders and with conditions on the Anzio beachhead becoming precarious, a compromise was finally worked out. The campaign in Italy was to have first call on resources in the Mediterranean. But Anvil was only to be postponed, not canceled, and planning was to move ahead. The situation was to be reviewed again on March 20.

For the moment, Anvil had received a reprieve, but its future remained uncertain. Already the Americans were contemplating a "delayed" French Riviera operation, and events during March tended to confirm the wisdom of this view. On the twenty-first and after a good deal of consultation with both sides, Eisenhower reached his decision: he was canceling Anvil as being simultaneous with Overlord.[17] In the same telegram and with the subsequent concurrence of the Combined Chiefs of Staff, he ordered that a number of the precious landing craft be reallocated immediately from the Mediterranean to England.

The British were elated with the decision. But as a concession to the Americans, they agreed to keep the Anvil option open. The British Chiefs said they held out the possibility of a future Anvil because they hoped the Allies would take Rome by June 15. At that point, the possibility of a landing in the south of France would once again become a viable op-

tion. For the present, then, Anvil had fallen victim to preparations for Normandy and fighting on the Italian front because as usual the Allies did not have overwhelming resources,
especially landing craft.

Nevertheless, detailed planning during the first three
months of 1944 had not been halted, and it proceeded apace.
Eisenhower's December appreciation, which his Allied Forces
Headquarters (AFHQ) planners had worked out, was now
turned over to the United States Seventh Army for more detailed work. They set up their staff at a schoolhouse just outside Algiers. It was a combined planning group, designated
Force 163, and it was placed under the overall direction of
General Clark. But since he was so heavily involved as commander of Fifth Army in Italy, actual supervision was exercised by United States Brig. Gen. Garrison H. Davidson.
Though constantly lamenting a lack of guidance from higher
headquarters, the planners did make a number of important
decisions.[18] With the help of naval experts who based their
thinking on the depth of the water immediately offshore (an
important factor in terms of mines as well as sea approaches),
the vehicle exits from the beaches, and the known enemy
defenses, the planning group decided that the "alternate"
site, the forty-five-mile stretch between the towns of Cavalaire-sur-Mer and Agay, was the best choice. They also confirmed that the 85th Infantry Division, training in North Africa, and the 3rd and 45th divisions, presently seeing combat
in Italy, were the most likely United States land units to be
involved. And while the French forces were not specifically
identified, they were expected to play a vital role and accordingly French advisors were brought into the planning process.

At the same time, in light of the Allied advance into Italy,
the Mediterranean theater was in the throes of being reorganized. British and American military leaders alike realized

the necessity of having a reorganization, even though Generals Devers and Eaker were dismayed with the Mediterranean situation after their own recent United Kingdom assignments, where everything "was tied up in a neat consolidated area and a marvelous logistic supporting establishment. Here everything is scattered form Hell to breakfast. It would be difficult to imagine a more widely dispersed area."[19]

The Italian peninsula was the key to the reorganization. Not only was it then the main combat area, but it was also beginning to serve as an additional base for air attacks aimed at Germany. Its location further offered the possibility of striking east, where Allied aircraft were already "supplying knives so that patriotic Balkans can cut a German throat or two," or west, where Anvil was being projected to take place. As Eaker summed it up in a February 19 letter to Col. George A. Brownell at the War Department in Washington: "The war has moved away from Africa and into Europe. We have, therefore to pick up and cut loose all the anchors we have been dragging in Africa and clean up our many logistic and communications establishments in Africa and consolidate them in Italy, the better to support the advance in Europe."[20]

While the theater reorganization was being carried through, the Force 163 planners were having their own difficulties. In part the problem was the unsure status of Anvil. But the main cause of concern was the lack of a commander on the spot. General Clark's commitment to the Italian campaign and to the Anzio operation in particular meant that he had little time left to oversee the planning for Anvil. Accordingly, on February 28, he was relieved of his responsibility for the southern France undertaking, and Lt. Gen. Alexander M. Patch, Jr., was appointed in his stead a few days later.

Although Patch's most recent assignment had been as head of IV Corps, stationed at Fort Lewis, Washington, he was best known for his command of the Guadalcanal campaign early in 1943, when it became primarily an army, rather than a marine, operation. Tall and angular, quiet yet forthright, "Sandy" Patch was considered a no-nonsense disciplinarian with a good grasp of strategy and tactics. He was a West Point graduate like his father, had fought in Europe in World War I, and then had served in various capacities in the interwar years. Soon after Pearl Harbor, he had helped defend New Caledonia in the Pacific from the Japanese. At the conclusion of the Guadalcanal operation, he had been brought home, some said because he had incurred General Marshall's displeasure. In fact, Marshall was upset by reports that Patch had inadvertently revealed secret information on code-breaking. But on having the matter investigated, Marshall found that the security breach was exaggerated and took no action against the colorful commander.[21]

Early in 1944 Patch was flown to North Africa to prepare his IV Corps for the Italian campaign. At this point the six-foot, accordian-playing, three-star general with close-cropped red hair entered the Seventh Army scene and became the driving force in the planning for Anvil. Commenting on his military capabilities, General Devers said of him after the war: "I knew him well . . . Patch was a fine commander, an excellent administrator, and he was also a good field commander because he knew tactics and strategy. He had a young staff and they were very aggressive. He worked well with supply units that I had."[22] Admiral Hewitt, the naval task force commander for Anvil was even more generous in his praise. When asked how it was to work with General Patch, he replied: "Splendid. Splendid. We developed a very good friendship right away. Of course, he was always insisting that the Navy . . . would never get the Army in the right place at the right time, or words to that effect, but that wherever we put him, he was going to go ashore and fight."[23]

Patch's appointment became official on March 5. He immediately set about coordinating Anvil with army and air force staff officers, but the Tentative Army Outline Plan of March 29 contained little that was new.[24] It was, after all, the culmination of the planning effort which had been set in motion eight months earlier. The operation was no longer contemplated as a three-, but as a two-division assault on selected French Riviera beaches between Cavalaire-sur-Mer and Agay. The initial landing force was to be preceded by airborne troops and commandos, who were delegated special tasks. All told ten divisions were to take part.

The subsequent tasks of the Anvil force also remained the same as in earlier planning. After establishing a beachhead by D + 1, Toulon was to be quickly captured. The American and French units were then to take Marseilles and move northward toward Lyons and Vichy. The main problem remained, of course, not when Anvil would take place, but whether it would ever be launched at all. Given other priorities and the continuing Anglo-American antagonism over the operation, it was conceivable that its temporary abandonment toward the end of March might become permanent.

2

German Strategy and Defenses

GERMAN THINKING ABOUT southern France began as early as the fall of France in June 1940. At that stage of the war, the Wehrmacht was concerned not so much about the possibility of a British invasion, which was considered quite remote, as it was about the political implications of occupying French soil. Despite an armistice agreement between the two sides, from the start, German officials viewed with some skepticism the new French regime, which had been installed at Vichy to administer the southeastern two-fifths of the country. In fact, in December 1940, under the guise of a possible revolt by Vichy French forces in the colonies, the Germans made plans to take over, if necessary, the rest of metropolitan France.

During the next two years relations between Hitler and the Vichy government varied between correct and strained. German plans for the occupation of southeastern France therefore remained in being, though hardly in a state of immediate readiness. By November 1942, however, the situation had deteriorated to the point that Hitler wanted to take over the region at the first possible opportunity. On the seventh, he indicated to the First Army, which was to direct the takeover, that he had decided to occupy by Blitz-type tactics the seat of the government at Vichy and the depot areas near the demarcation line between occupied and unoccupied France.[1] He was doing this, as he put it, "to prevent enemy agitation and putsch attempts in the unoccupied zone." The Fuehrer order went on to say that "an occupation of the entire unoccupied area . . . might be undertaken according to the situation."

Although it surprised the Germans, the Allies' amphibious invasion of Northwest Africa on the eighth presented them with the opportunity. Preparations for Anton, as the German operation was called, were set in motion, though Wehrmacht units did not cross the demarcation line. Hitler wanted to wait several days before moving to see what the reaction of the Vichy forces in North Africa would be. But with French military resistance collapsing and with a number of supposedly loyal Vichy officials and commanders in Morocco and Algeria demonstrating at best an attitude of duplicity, Hitler decided to act. On November 10 he ordered Anton to proceed.[2]

At seven o'clock the next morning, German forces began moving into the unoccupied zone. Three divisions under First Army—the 7th Panzer, 327th Infantry, and SS "Death's Head" divisions—made rapid progress from the west. Three more divisions—the 10th Panzer, 328th Infantry, and 335th Infantry—under Army Task Force Felber, named after its commander, General of the Infantry Hans Felber, pushed across the demarcation line in the north. Resistance from the 100,000-man French armistice army or from the citizenry at large did not materialize. By seven that evening, 7th Panzer had reached Toulouse, 160 miles from the starting line. Early the next day, the 7th, along with 10th Panzer, continued their advance to the Mediterranean coast. Soon afterwards infantry troops began arriving by rail in Marseilles and also started moving into towns west of the Rhône River. At the same time, specially designated German units took over supply depots and ammunition dumps in the rear and occupied border posts along the boundary with Spain, while the Luftwaffe assumed control of the airfields in the area. Though it did not attempt to occupy the harbors, the German Navy made sure that French ships did not escape to Allied or neutral ports.

In the meantime, just after noon on the eleventh, four divisions of the Italian Fourth Army advanced west along the French Riviera coastline and also into the mountainous interior east of the Rhône. In addition, one division sailed from Genoa and another one from Sardinia toward Corsica. After encountering rough seas, they occupied the island the next day. In just two days, and with almost no casualties, all of southeastern France, including the Mediterranean coast, had fallen under German and Italian control.

The occupation was still far from complete, however. In spite of the detailed plans that had been worked out beforehand, a number of questions had still not been resolved. There was, for example, the matter of disarming the French forces, and especially of replacing the personnel who manned the artillery pieces which rimmed the coast. At first the German field commanders allowed some of the French troops to retain their arms and the artillery units to remain at their guns. But by the nineteenth Hitler had become so disenchanted with the Vichy military leaders that he declared, "After the treachery in North Africa, the reliability of the French troops can no longer be guaranteed."[3] He therefore decided "to disarm the French Army and Air Force (including the coastal artillery) and allow only the police and some of the border guards" to retain their weapons. Accordingly, the French Army was relieved of its firearms, withdrawn into the interior, and eventually disbanded.

Moreover, German and Italian areas of responsibility along the coast had not been clearly delineated. Originally the Italians had been expected to control the entire coastline east of the Rhône to the Italian border. But this would leave both the naval base at Toulon and the main commercial port, Marseilles, in Italian hands. After the occupation, Commander-in-Chief West, Field Marshal Gerd von Rundstedt, went so far as to request that the entire French Mediterranean coast be placed under German command. Hitler rejected the request, but he eventually allowed German forces to retain Marseilles, including 158 French merchant ships moored in the harbor.[4]

Even more crucial was the status of Toulon. Toulon had been a major French naval base for centuries, and it had become the focal point of the Vichy French navy after France's defeat in June 1940. Although at the time Hitler greatly desired to have the world's fourth largest fleet under his control, he realized that the French, so recently allied with Britain, would refuse to go that far. And they might, if provoked, even set sail for British ports. As part of the armistice agreement, therefore, he guaranteed the fleet's neutrality.

In November of 1942 it was still a considerable force of some eighty ships in varying stages of repair. It included three battleships (two of them of older vintage), seven cruisers, a seaplane carrier, twenty-nine destroyers, and twenty submarines. At the time of the occupation, the French navy reaffirmed its intention to remain neutral, and the Germans reiterated their pledge to respect French desires. By the seventeenth, however, Hitler had decided that Toulon, this "unoccupied zone in miniature," must come under Axis domination. The 7th Panzer Division, then on the coast near the Spanish border, was delegated the task. By the twenty-fifth, German planners, headed by SS Gen. Paul Hausser and headquartered at a hotel in Aix-en-Provence, had assembled the necessary forces for the operation, which was code named Lila. They realized that the possibility of taking over the French fleet intact was indeed a slim one, but they felt they must take the chance. At least the fear of French vessels escaping to Allied or neutral ports would now be brought to an end.

Lila was scheduled to take place before dawn on the twenty-seventh.[5] At four o'clock in the morning four battle groups, reinforced by special forces, including a motorcycle brigade and naval units to take over the ships, began moving swiftly into the city and toward the harbor area. The French, who had given part of their crews overnight liberty for the first time since November 8, were surprised, but not overcome. Although the Germans were able to silence most of the communications points in the city, one duty officer, Lt. Comdr. Paul Le Nabec, was able to telephone and alert French officers at the harbor of Germany's attempt to storm the port. By 5:55, when the first German units began to arrive at the main docks, French crews were already in the process of scuttling their ships. The Germans could do little but watch helplessly from the quays.

Adm. Paul Auphan and Jacques Mordal in their book on the French navy gave a graphic illustration of what happened. When a German battle group commander reached the cruiser *Algérie*, the necessary actions had been carried out, and it was on the verge of sinking. The admiral and his flag captain were standing on the pier.

"We have come to take over your ship," announced the German officer.

"You are a little late," answered the French admiral. "It is already sinking."

"Will it blow up?"

"No."

"In that case," said the German, "we will go aboard."

"In that case," replied the Frenchman, "it will blow up." Scenes such as these were repeated all over the dock area. By the time the whole harbor was in German hands at 8:30, only twelve ships remained afloat (four destroyers, two submarines, and six minesweepers).

Nevertheless, both the Germans and the Italians considered the raid a success. The Italians were able to raise more than thirty vessels in the ensuing months, and several of them saw action before Italy concluded an armistice with the Allies in September 1943. The Germans were pleased that only four ships—all of them submarines—had escaped to neutral or Allied ports, and, more importantly, that the last vestige of unoccupied France was now under direct Axis control.

But the November occupation had its negative side as well. Four hundred additional miles of coastline—275 German and 125 Italian—now had to be defended against a possible enemy attack. This not only necessitated more troops, but naval and air force unit as well. Besides military personnel, the Germans hoped to divert Organization Todt workers (many of them foreign) from other tasks to improve the existing defenses and build up new ones along the coast. At the same time the situation at Stalingrad and in North Africa had reached crisis proportions, thus imposing additional strains on the German war machine. Axis domination of southern France, though considered necessary, could not have come at a more unpropitious time.

At the end of November the Fuehrer felt that an Allied invasion threat (which he had never believed serious anyway) had passed, and German commanders began to impose a defensive framework over the former Vichy zone. Field Marshal von Rundstedt, as head of the western theater, which now included all of France as well as Belgium and the Netherlands, assumed overall command. Army Task Force Felber with its headquarters at Avignon took over tactical control of the German-held coastal stretch along the Mediterranean, while First Army returned to Bordeaux to look after France's Atlantic coast. The occupation forces under Military Commander, France, extended their duties from northern France to the southern interior as well as providing border guards for the Pyrenees boundary with Spain. And the Italian Fourth Army with four divisions under General Vercellino remained in its sector, including Toulon, east of the Rhône.

Even though conditions in the area had stabilized, the surface calm belied a good deal of activity. As one might expect, the German formations which had taken part in the occupation, including the 7th and 10th Panzer divisions, returned to their former positions or moved out to other, more endangered fronts. The three divisions which took over defense of the coast—the 326th, 338th, and 356th Infantry—plus the one in reserve were new formations which lacked sufficient training and heavy artillery pieces.[6] By July 1943, the situation had improved to the extent that these divisions, with a total of 57,818 troops, were considered adequate for coastal defense tasks. But except for the 60th Panzer Grenadier Division "Feldherrnhalle," which was in reserve, they did not possess sufficient vehicles for offensive assignments.

The Wehrmacht had also begun to make use of the existing artillery pieces along the coast, training crews to man them. Most of the 108 army and naval coastal guns (with a range varying between four and thirty miles) were grouped around the ports, especially Marseilles, but only eleven of them were not of French, Czech, or Russian make.[7] These, combined with ninety-one pieces of divisional artillery (range between five and eight miles), were not under cover and thought to be insufficient to defend the 275-mile coastline. Nevertheless, the deficiencies in artillery pieces (and other weapons) for the coast were slowly being made good by deliveries from the Reich and other places in Occupied Europe.

The deficiencies in the number of fortifications proved even more intractable. The Germans made plans, undertook inspections, and engaged French firms as well as ones from the Reich. They also detailed some engineering troops and Organization Todt laborers to begin the work. But their accomplishments were meager, especially when compared with the main construction effort in the west—the Atlantic Wall.

Still the Germans were attempting to establish at least the semblance of a defensive posture along their portion of the French Mediterranean coast. Curiously enough, their efforts were brought to a halt, not directly by the British and American enemies, but by the defection of their ally, Italy. The Italian forces had been deteriorating for some months. German staff officers at higher headquarters as early as May and June of 1943 noted the symptoms and anticipated that the Italians might even capitulate. In that event, they realized that German units would have to be moved quickly into Italian-held territory in the Balkans and southeastern France as well as down the Italian peninsula. With the successful Allied invasion of Sicily and then the overthrow of Mussolini by the Fascist Council on July 24, the Germans began to take definite steps to implement a takeover. In fact, at the end of July it looked as if Wehrmacht formations might occupy Italian territory at any moment.[8]

Marshal Pietro Badoglio, who had replaced Mussolini as head of the government thus found himself in an almost untenable position. The Italians greatly desired to get out of the war. But in their weakened condition, they could hardly refuse any legitimate demands their German ally made upon the government. Not only was there the possibility of a German occupation, but there was also the fear of reprisals against the Italian populace itself. Italian officials therefore chose the alternative of engaging in secret armistice talks with the Allies while at the same time allowing the Germans to ease into Italian-controlled territory with the least amount of bloodshed possible.

In the Italian zone east of the Rhône, the Germans undertook a number of specific moves during August. All of them, however, stopped short of complete occupation. The Fourth Italian Army permitted six German divisions from the west to come through their area on the way to Italy. The Italian commanders, many of whom were understandably sympathetic toward Germany, also allowed German army, naval, and air units to establish an "increased presence" at major harbors and airfields in their sector. And they did nothing to prevent portions of four divisions under neighboring Army Task Force Felber, which was renamed Nineteenth Army after its fifty-four-year-old leader had departed to another command in the Balkans, from moving into the region "to support our Italian allies."

These measures involved considerable improvisation, but by the twentieth the Germans had reached an agreement with the Italian High Command to ease the transition of control in the area.[9] Despite some last minute friction between the two sides, a peaceful occupation began on August 29. Indicative of their cooperation was a meeting on the thirty-first, in which the Italian and German staffs immediately involved had come together to iron out any problems which still remained.[10] At the dinner which followed, the new Nineteenth Army commander, Gen. Georg von Sodenstern, thanked the Italain hosts for their hospitality and comradeship, and the commander of the Fourth Italian Army, General Vercellino, responded in an equally cordial (*herzlich*) manner. Given this atmosphere, it is little wonder that, by the time the Italian government announced an armistice on September 8, measures for effecting the occupation were already well advanced.

That same evening, having received the code word Axis, German forces already in the Italian zone officially began to take over and disarm the Italian troops who still remained there.[11] The 356th Infantry, with the help of naval units, occupied the coastline in and around Toulon. Farther east, the 715th Infantry Division, temporarily motorized, established control over the area from Cavalaire-sur-Mer to east of Cannes, while Panzer Grenadier Division "Feldherrnhalle" took over the coastal region nearest to Italy and the mountain passes along the border.

The only trouble for the Germans occurred farther north at the Mont Cenis railway tunnel, a link between Lyons and Turin in northern Italy.[12] Nineteenth Army assigned the task of taking over the tunnel to Battle Group Münch, which was detached from the 715th Infantry, and to a regiment of the 157th Reserve Division located at Grenoble. When Major Münch and his force arrived in the area on the afternoon of the ninth, some of the Italian soldiers and their commanders refused to be disarmed and proceeded to blow up and block portions of the tunnel. During the night and throughout the next day, sporadic fighting broke out between the two sides. By the evening of the tenth, however, the Germans had finally secured the entire region. In the aftermath, the Germans detailed 400 of the 1,000 Italian troops who were rounded up to repair the damages, a job which required at least two weeks to complete.

In all, 41,057 Italians were captured in southeastern France and separated into three groups.[13] Those who wished to continue fighting on the German side numbered about

1,400 soldiers and were given over to combat units. By far the largest number—around 29,500—agreed to serve with the German armed forces, but only as noncombatants. They were generally parceled out among various military engineering and supply units in France and the Low Countries. The other more than 10,000 prisoners were considered interns and were transported to the Reich for work in the armament factories.

Even though all of southern France was now under German control, conditions were scarcely better than had been the case ten months earlier when German and Italian forces had first occupied the area. One-hundred twenty-five miles of Mediterranean shoreline had been added to Germany's defense commitments. While the Italians had made some effort to improve the defenses in their zone, the Germans considered them far from adequate, especially in terms of too few soldiers and workers, insufficient coastal artillery guns, and almost nonexistent antitank walls. Even Marseilles and Toulon, though well defended from the sea, did not possess sufficient fortifications on the landward side for effective all-around defense. And in another far-reaching Allied move, Free French forces had taken Corsica in September and early October.

The Wehrmacht thus found itself stretched to the limit in southern France, and little help could be expected from other quarters. Trying to prevent British and American forces from advancing up the Italian boot was difficult enough, but this, combined with attempts to combat the Soviet advance in the east and the increasingly devastating Allied bomber offensive from the west, made the German situation even more tenuous in the fall of 1943. This meant that German commanders along France's Mediterranean coast could expect little assistance, and in fact could anticipate having to give up their best forces to other theaters.

The inevitable was not long in coming. The Armed Forces High Command ordered three divisions—the 356th Infantry, Panzer Grenadier "Feldherrnhalle," and 10th SS Panzer (the latter having been held in reserve during the takeover of the Italian zone)—to begin pulling out of the area. Their replacements were three understrength, immobile divisions capable only of assuming coastal defense duties. In addition, considerable numbers of Eastern battalions, fighting for Germany, but made up of Azerbaijanis, Turkomans, and other Russian nationalities, started to appear for the first time in southern France. As a further sign of declining manpower, on November 20, almost 20 percent (10,000 out of 48,000) of the soldiers in the region were Germans from the Reich who were under nineteen or over thirty-seven years of age.

Nevertheless, at this same time, in the fall of 1943, a movement in the opposite direction began, a movement designed to strengthen—and quickly—Germany's defensive posture in the west. This effort was to include, at least to an extent, southern France. A strongly worded fifty-page situation report sent by Field Marshal von Rundstedt to Hitler on October 28 initiated the call for action.[14] In it, Rundstedt pointed out that the long-anticipated Anglo-American invasion of western Europe was in the offing for 1944, and that all available resources had to be brought together and readied as soon as possible for the impending attack. Less than a week later the Fuehrer issued his own directive, in which he declared:

> The threat from the East remains, but an even greater danger looms in the West: the Anglo-American landing! . . . If the enemy here succeeds in penetrating our defenses on a wide front, consequences of staggering proportions will follow within a short time. All signs point to an offensive . . . no later than

spring, and perhaps earlier. For that reason I can no longer jus-
tify the further weakening of the West in favor of other theaters
of war. I have therefore decided to strengthen the defenses in
the West.[15]

It took several months for Hitler's directive to achieve any
tangible results, but by the end of 1943 the western buildup
had started in earnest. Most of the activity centered around
the English Channel coast, which had always been considered, for obvious reasons, the most likely area for an Allied
landing. It was within range of Allied fighter aircraft and
also provided the most direct route to the heart of Germany
and the Ruhr industrial area.

But German calculations did not completely exclude the
French Mediterranean coast either. They felt that the Allies
would in all likelihood attempt more than one landing. In
this case a separate Mediterranean attack might be anticipated as a diversionary action or as a secondary invasion designed eventually to link up with the main assault along the
Channel. The local commanders realized that in spite of the
efforts over the past year, the problems to be overcome in
the Mediterranean sector were formidable. And they had
little assurance that the difficulties could be surmounted in
time, if at all. This did not mean that the Germans intended
to give up. During the next five months, from the beginning
of 1944 until the Normandy landings, they made every effort
to build up their defensive system. This effort focused on
three areas: increased manpower, firepower, and fortifications.

The manpower problem proved especially troublesome.
On the surface, the Germans could point to considerable
progress.[16] In December 1943, only two corps, with five divisions under them, were responsible for defending the
coast, and one partially motorized division was held in re-

serve. Six months later the number had risen to three corps, seven divisions along the coast, with two panzer divisions in reserve, and the length of coastline each division had to defend had been reduced considerably. Yet this apparent overall improvement masked a number of difficulties. Two of the six divisions located in the area in December—the 326th and 715th Infantry divisions—were moved out to meet crises in Italy and on the Eastern Front. Of the four that remained, three—the 244th, 242nd, and 148th Reserve divisions—had only recently been formed and had to be brought up to strength. The other division—the 338th Infantry—had been stationed in the region since early 1943, but it still lacked sufficient infantry troops. The same situation applied to the three new coastal divisions that began arriving in January 1944. The 271st, 272nd, and 277th Infantry divisions were new formations which lacked personnel, experience, weapons, and mobility.

To make up for the shortages, the Germans increasingly had to rely upon older Germans (those over thirty-eight) and foreign troops as well as young recruits. By June almost all of the six Eastern battalions in the area were deployed along the coast. Many of the older soldiers were designated fortress troops and assigned to look after the artillery guns in and around Marseilles and Toulon. Even the two panzer divisions in reserve, though a vast improvement over the situation earlier, were subject to manning and equipment deficiencies. Having suffered heavy losses on the Russian front, on June 1, they were still in the process of being filled out. The 9th Panzer Division, with its headquarters at Avignon, had only 12,768 troops (instead of its normal quota of around 17,000), making it the smallest of the ten armored divisions in the West. The 2nd SS Division "Das Reich," which was located at Toulouse so that it could be shifted east or west, was supposed to have a total of 163 tanks. Instead, it only had 44

Mark IVs and 25 Mark V Panthers for a total of 69. Furthermore, the Germans never attained the number of divisions they considered necessary to defend the area properly: eight to ten along the entire coast with three more as a tactical reserve, plus two to three panzer divisions as a strategic reserve. Even taking into account all of the difficulties and shortages, however, the overall manpower situation had obviously improved appreciably since the first of the year.

During this time the Germans set in motion another change which they hoped would improve their chances of driving the Allied invasion, when it came, into the sea: they reorganized their command structure. Instead of dealing directly with Field Marshal von Rundstedt as Commander-in-Chief West, an intervening command—Army Task Force G—was now interposed between Nineteenth Army and the theater commander. This move made it possible for von Rundstedt to oversee the entire theater, placated Field Marshal Erwin Rommel of Afrika Korps fame who assumed control of the Channel sector as head of Army Group B, and brought all of southern France from the Atlantic to the Italian border under a single tactical command, Army Task Force G. (A task force functioned like an army group, but had fewer staff personnel.) Named to lead the task force was Gen. Johannes Blaskowitz.

Blaskowitz, like von Rundstedt, was a holdover from the old imperial army. Born in East Prussia in 1883, he had become a second lieutenant in 1902 and had later served in World War I as a company and battalion commander and as a general staff officer. Between the wars he occupied various command positions and served on the General Staff as the Inspector for Weapons Schools.

Early in World War II, Blaskowitz had been groomed for a top command assignment. In the Polish campaign he had led Eighth Army, was then promoted to the rank of colonel general (the equivalent of a four-star general), and placed in charge of Theater Command East with its headquarters in Warsaw. But during the fall of 1939 he incurred Hitler's wrath by indicating in a memorandum his disgust with the behavior and activities of SS personnel in Poland. (It is ironic that after the war he was accused of mistreating Polish POWs and civilians and was arraigned to stand trial at Nuremberg. Just before his trial was to open in 1948, Blaskowitz leaped from a catwalk in the Nuremberg prison and killed himself.) As a result of Hitler's displeasure, he was relegated to heading a reserve army during the battle of France and was then demoted further to commanding the relatively quiet First Army sector along France's Bay of Biscay coast. Only with the Army Task Force G assignment was he once again given the possibility of serving in an active, frontline command.

As a military leader, he was considered a sound tactician with a thorough grasp of the various aspects of command. Though perhaps overstated, Gen. Bodo Zimmermann, von Rundstedt's operations officer, described Blaskowitz after the war as follows: "In his conception and his mode of life, Colonel General Blaskowitz [had] . . . a strong spiritual and religious turn of mind. Rigorously just and high-minded, at the beginning of the war he protested against the General Government (the German administration in central Poland). Relieved of his command and in open disfavor, . . . he always remained the straightforward soldier who wanted to do his duty simply for the sake of his Fatherland and his people."[17]

By the time Blaskowitz and his staff took over tactical direction of the French Mediterranean coast in May, they could point not only to some improvement in terms of personnel, but also to a substantial increase in the number of artillery pieces on hand.[18] In late 1942, just after German forces had occupied the western portion of the Vichy zone, only 199 artillery pieces had been in their area. By June 1944, the number had more than tripled to 666 guns.

To be sure, the increase is in some ways misleading. The Germans had 125 miles of additional coastline to defend. More than half of the guns, 337, were light artillery pieces (between 75 and 120 mm), and 53 of the 60 coastal batteries (two of them were railway guns) consisted of guns of foreign make. But the German effort still represented a considerable advance over the situation eighteen, or even five, months earlier.

While little help was forthcoming in the air and naval spheres (the navy barely had enough ships for harbor defense), the German buildup of its coastal defenses was also quite impressive.[19] At the end of January 1944, they had constructed 341 permanent fortifications; by June, 942 had been completed. Most of the work was accomplished by Organization Todt laborers, who built them out of reinforced concrete according to a standardized design, thus making for rapid construction. In addition, German troops themselves helped by erecting numerous field-type defenses, such as earthen embankments, antitank ditches, slit trenches, barbed wire entanglements, and the like. Antilanding stakes, foreshore obstacles (which workmen had to lay in the water because there was little difference between high and low tide), and 62,486 land and sea mines added further to the defensive appearance of the landscape. Evacuation of French civilians from the coast was also stepped up, and the Germans proceeded to take over buildings and seaside villas and conceal big guns in them. As a finishing touch, German engineering troops flooded a low lying area near the mouth of the Rhône deemed especially suitable for an Allied landing.

All of this effort began to come apart with the Normandy invasion. To be sure, Organization Todt continued its work, especially at several vital bauxite mines in the interior, but only under increased protection. In the meantime troop and equipment levels in the south declined markedly in the wake of the Allied D Day assault. Three infantry divisions which had recently been brought up to strength—the 271st, the 272nd, and 277th—were moved out in July.[20] Their replacements were the 716th Infantry, which had been badly mauled in Normandy; the 198th Infantry, which had suffered a similar fate on the Russian front and was in the process of being reformed; and the 189th Reserve Division, which had been used mainly for training purposes in the interior of France.

The Allied breakout toward the end of July precipitated another crisis. Field Marshal Günther von Kluge, who had replaced von Rundstedt as Commander-in-Chief West, asked for additional help from the south, this time from the 242nd Infantry Division. But the Armed Forces High Command turned down his request. Nineteenth Army did respond, however, by combing out 800 additional troops from other units in the South, and hurriedly dispatched four motorized artillery battalions and antitank and antiaircraft guns north to try and stem the United States breakout near Saint-Lô.

Even worse from Blaskowitz's standpoint was the loss of two of his three panzer divisions. The 2nd SS Panzer departed from Toulouse in June, and the 9th Panzer followed suit toward the end of July. This left only one armored formation in all of southern France (and von Kluge also wanted it shifted north). The 11th Panzer was moved from Bordeaux to Toulouse so that it could meet an Allied attack aimed either at the Bay of Biscay or the Mediterranean coasts. But its presence alone was obviously inadequate. The best higher headquarters could promise was that a worn-out fast division (not necessarily armored) would be sent to the area sometime in the future.

At the same time, pressure from the French Resistance reached alarming proportions. The Resistance, in spite of its disparate nature, had always been strongest in the former Vichy zone, and numbered as many as 15,000 persons in June of 1944. When the Normandy landings took place the incidence of sabotage acts, as the Germans called them, rose dramatically. Besides the usual cutting of telegraph and telephone lines, destruction of bridges, and disruption of the supply network in general, "travel," according to a German commission responsible for overseeing conditions in southern France "outside of cities and areas controlled by the Wehrmacht was possible only under heavy escort."[21] Army Task Force G on July 7 indicated that the rail line between Toulouse and Saint-Gaudens, a distance of some sixty miles, had been cut in thirty-eight places. Another report stated that on the night of July 18 a freight train traveling through the mountains of central France was stopped by 150 armed terrorists and searched to see if German soldiers or equipment were on board. Blazkowitz wired Commander-in-Chief West on the twenty-eighth: "The activity of bands in the rear of the Army Task Force has been allowed gradually to reach the point that control over a greater part of the area can no longer be referred to. Only where German troops are in evidence can peace and order be preserved."[22]

In this atmosphere the German response to the Resistance bands became increasingly shrill. Not only were security forces engaged against the French (and the Allied specialists who had been flown in), but portions of the armored formations became involved as well. The 9th Panzer, for instance, just before being sent north, swept through an area east of the Rhône and claimed thirty-six enemy dead plus a large number of weapons and much ammunition captured. Its own losses were four dead and twelve wounded.

A particularly tragic event occurred on the Vercors plateau southwest of Grenoble, where, according to the British official historian, 20,000 German troops trapped 4,000 French Maquis shortly after D Day.[23] The resisters held out in the mountain stronghold for over a month in the expectation of receiving desperately needed supplies. Some finally arrived in the form of an Allied airdrop on July 14, Bastille Day. The French demonstrated their elation (and defiance) by proclaiming their bastion the "Free Republic of the Vercors." On the twenty-first, gliders arrived, supposedly carrying reinforcements as well as additional supplies. But they turned out to be crack SS troops who made quick work of the beleaguered Frenchmen. Meanwhile, the Resistance movement had been dealt a further blow a week earlier when eighteen of its leaders along with twenty-six others were betrayed and captured while holding a meeting north of Aix-en-Provence.

The Germans were well aware that all of this activity in southern France could not be attributed solely to the Normandy invasion. Besides the Resistance measures, reports from German agents, deciphered enemy messages, and increased British and United States air and naval activity all pointed in the direction of another attack. Theater officers expected the attack to take place along France's Mediterranean coast. On July 3, Army Task Force G indicated that an enemy landing attempt was probable. By the end of the month German staff officers were convinced that the probability would become a reality, though they had not yet pinpointed the exact time and place.

The situation in the south became even more precarious with the Allied breakout in the north. Although still not an accomplished fact, the Wehrmacht realized that a rapid Allied advance across France could well cut off German forces guarding the Bay of Biscay and Mediterranean coasts. Col. Gen. Alfred Jodl, the operations officer at Armed Forces

High Command headquarters and a key advisor to Hitler, went so far as to contemplate withdrawing German units from the area altogether, but then decided such a move was premature.

By August 1, 1944, an overall deterioration in southern France had therefore already set in. While seven infantry divisions still rimmed the Mediterranean coast, they were generally undermanned, underequipped, inexperienced formations capable only of limited offensive operations. General of the Infantry Friedrich Wiese, commander of Nineteenth Army, could call on two divisions in reserve—the 11th Panzer at Toulouse and the 157th Reserve Division at Grenoble. But both were a long way from the probable battle area, and only the 11th Panzer was equipped so as to be of immediate use.

German naval forces were considered of little consequence, for they consisted of one destroyer (at Genoa), seven submarines, five torpedo boats, seven escort vessles, thirty PT boats, and approximately thirty auxiliary ships.[24] The air force had only about 65 bombers (JU 88s), 30 fighters, and 35 reconnaissance aircraft, or 130 in all, in the immediate area ready for action. Even though the Germans still had over 600 artillery pieces placed along the coast, the loss of antitank and antiaircraft guns could not help but have had a further adverse effect on their defensive capabilities.

These factors, combined wit the anticipated Allied assault and staggering defeats on other fronts, did not bode well for German prospects of repelling an invasion. In a classic understatement, General Blaskowitz signaled Field Marshal von Kluge on August 2, "The strength of Nineteenth Army no longer guarantees a successful defense of the coast."[25]

3

Anvil Becomes Dragoon

T HE ALLIED postponement of Anvil on March 21 did not eliminate it from being considered a viable option. In fact, United States military leaders continued to express their determination that Anvil be implemented. On March 22, Brig. Gen. George A. Lincoln, one of the top army planners in Washington, sent his boss, Maj. Gen. Frank N. Roberts, a memorandum entitled "What Shall We Do About Anvil?" In it, he ably summarized the American view.[1] If the Allies did not conduct an operation in southern France, Lincoln pointed out:

1. We get into political difficulties with the French.

2. Overlord remains woefully short of fighting divisions for the battle which may have to be fought in France.

3. Our service forces will continue to support the Western Mediterranean.

4. Our divisions and the French divisions will be committed to a costly, unremunerative, inching advance in Italy. The home people of both the United States and France may or may not take this indefinitely.

5. Once committed to Italy, we have our forces pointed

towards the Balkans and will have the greatest difficulty in preventing their use for occupation forces in Austria, Hungary, and Southern Germany.

On the twenty-fourth, the American Joint Chiefs forwarded to their British counterparts a memo which reflected Lincoln's position as well as other military developments that had occurred during the past several weeks.[2] The Joint Chiefs agreed that Anvil should be postponed and that landing craft be released from the Mediterranean for Overlord. But they still contended that Anvil should eventually be launched on a two-divisional assault basis. The new target date, in their opinion, should be July 10. To make their recommendation more palatable, the Americans said they would be willing (supposedly at great sacrifice) to divert sixty-six landing craft, originally scheduled for Pacific operations, for use in the Mediterranean.

At first the British were elated with the American offer, for they presumed that they could use the landing craft for *any* Mediterranean operation they wished. To their way of thinking this meant using them to press the campaign in Italy. However, the Americans soon made it clear that the landing craft were not being made available for just any Mediterranean operation; they wanted them earmarked specifically for Anvil.

The deadlock between the two allies, which continued into April, did not reach critical proportions in part because each side exhibited a good deal of forbearance toward the other. But mainly it was because the British and Americans had other commitments, namely Overlord and Italy, which they rightly judged to be of more immediate concern than Anvil. Overlord was in its final stages of preparation, and nothing they felt should be done to predjudice its execution, now scheduled for early June. The situation in Italy remained tense. Troops in the Anzio bridgehead had still not linked up with the main Allied force, and an operation designed to accomplish this had had to be put off from April until mid-May. The British therefore contended that at this point withdrawing forces from Italy for Anvil made no sense.[3] In their view, until the Italian offensive began, Rome was taken, and a defensive line established across central Italy, an operation aimed at southern France was out of the question.

The American response on April 8 was curt and to the point. The Joint Chiefs canceled forthwith their offer to send landing craft to the Mediterranean.[4] By the eighteenth, however, tempers had cooled, and a compromise directive of sorts had been worked out. As Matloff points out, while the directive mentioned neither the target date for Anvil nor additional assault craft, the Americans did agree to support with all of their resources the impending offensive in Italy.[5] The British, for their part, conceded that plans and preparations for Anvil, or for other possible operations to assist Overlord, should be pushed forward as vigorously as possible.

Thus, Anvil still remained a possibility. On April 19, Field Marshal Sir Alan Brooke, the head of the British Chiefs of Staff, recorded in his diary (with more than a trace of bitterness): "At last our troubles about Anvil are over. We have got the Americans to agree, but have lost the additional landing craft they were to provide. History will never forgive them for bargaining equipment against strategy and for trying to blackmail us into agreeing with them by holding the pistol of withdrawing craft at our heads."[6]

Many of the issues which supposedly stood in the way of Anvil being executed were resolved in late April and during May. On April 28, the United States Joint Chiefs showed their determination for launching Anvil by having Admiral King, the United States Chief of Naval Operations, whose brusque manner and advocacy of Pacific operations often put him at odds with Britain's military leaders, renew the American proposal to provide landing craft for the operation.[7] At the same time he added that they might even be used for some amphibious assault other than Anvil. The British quickly accepted King's offer, and by May 8 the details had been agreed upon. The United States would send to the Mediterranean nineteen LSTs, each one carrying an LCT. The first nine LSTs were to arrive by June 20, the remainder by a month later.

The British Chiefs of Staff sent instructions to Field Marshal Wilson which further strengthened Anvil's status, but not because it was their original intention to do so. On April 25, they had directed Wilson to look into other amphibious operations which might be undertaken once the fronts in Italy were joined. He had his planners examine the feasibility of four possible seaborne operations: near Sète, west of the Rhône; east of Toulon (Anvil); near Genoa in northwestern Italy; and north of Rome. In the meantime, Churchill revived another amphibious project, an assault against France's western Bay of Biscay coast. While the United States Joint Chiefs, with Wilson's help, beat back Churchill's latest scheme, on May 17 Wilson notified the British Chiefs that he was "of the opinion that, in order to effect entry of a substantial force, with the assault lift which will now be available, at the earliest stage of decreasing German resistance, the most promising area in Southern France is that at present selected for operation Anvil."[8] In the same telegram, he also discussed the possible timing for the operation and concluded that it could be launched sometime between mid-August and mid-September. American commanders in the Mediterranean for the most part agreed with Wilson, though, reflecting Washington's thinking, they considered the mid-August date as the more plausible of the two.

Toward the end of May, Anvil was therefore much closer to realization than ever before. The Americans were sending precious landing craft to the Mediterranean. Planners had once again examined other possibilities for an amphibious attack and had decided that none of them held the attraction of a Provençal invasion east of Toulon. Just as importantly, Wilson and the British Chiefs in London seemed to concur with the decision. They also supported the idea of attempting to launch the operation by August 15 or a little later. With developments in Italy now taking a turn for the better—the Allied offensive, begun in mid-May, had led to a joining of the two fronts south of Rome on May 25—Anvil's prospects for being executed were brighter than ever.

At the same time, the French contribution of manpower and know-how, long considered essential for the operation's success, began to come more into play. During the spring, Force 163 planners had benefited a good deal from French expertise and advice. Not only had French staff officers, with their intimate knowledge of the Provençal coast and the topography inland been helpful, but French Resistance fighters were sending out increasingly accurate tactical intelligence information as well.

In addition, the French combat role started to take definite shape. Free French forces consisted primarily of Frenchmen from Metropolitan France and North Africa (*colons*), but they also included a number of African troops. Some of the French units (comprising land, naval, and air force formations) had already, under British and United States direction, seen extensive combat during the North African campaigns in 1942 and 1943. By the end of 1943, the French were in the process of having eleven divisions armed and equipped (in some cases reequipped) by the Americans for eventual use on the European continent. In January two divisions—the 2nd Moroccan and 3rd Algerian Infantry divisions—had been sent to Italy, and by May the equivalent of nearly five divisions (105,000 troops) were there.[9] Most of these forces were expected at some future date to participate in Anvil.

The most important element still missing was an overall French commander. In April, De Gaulle selected Gen. Jean de Lattre de Tassigny for the position. General de Lattre's military career was typical of many high-ranking French officers. Born in 1889, he had attended Saint-Cyr military academy, served in World War I, and then held a variety of staff and command assignments during the interwar years. During the battle of France, he was chief of staff for the Fifth Army and after the French defeat, he held several different command positions in the 100,000-man armistice army.

At this point his career diverged from that of other regular officers. Always loyal to the cause of France, he personally decided to resist when the Germans and Italians took over the Vichy sector in November 1942. The Germans responded by arresting him and sentencing him to ten years' imprisonment. He tried to escape on four different occasions during the next ten months, and finally succeeded in October 1943 and made his way to England. According to his own account, he arrived in North Africa on December 20, 1943, and was asked to take command of the Second Free French Army a month later. From that position it was only a short step to being named head of the French forces for the projected Anvil operation.

One of the most perceptive assessments of General de Lattre comes from Capt. Sir Basil Liddell Hart, the late British military expert. He asserts that de Lattre was exacting and a hard driver, yet he picked young subordinates of ability and allowed them to argue points of strategy with him. He also had a flair for the dramatic in public. But as Liddell Hart records, "In private I never saw the least trace of theatricality, while in numerous confidential talks I was struck by the absence of the signs of vanity which most famous men reveal, however well they conceal it in public." In sum, "He had dynamism and creative imagination, the two most essential qualities for supreme command."[10]

Despite de Lattre's appointment and expressions of good will among the French and their United States and British allies, tensions were bound to occur. One of the problems revolved around the mundane matter of difficulties over language (particularly for the Americans). Another problem was that the Free French movement was as much political as it was military in orientation. De Gaulle had had to overcome numerous difficulties at the beginning, and only now, in the spring of 1944, was he becoming accepted as the leader of a new France. In this sense, he was obviously very much concerned about maintaining as well as expanding his political authority. Most important from France's standpoint was the "shame of 1940." The stigma of defeat had dealt the French military a heavy blow. To be sure, a portion of the blame could be placed on the British. But the fact still remained, France had collapsed, Britain had not. The aggressive demeanor exhibited by the Free French leaders is therefore understandable in part because of their desire for France to regain her military honor.

A further divisive issue between the Americans and their French ally was over who should command Anvil. Even though General Patch had been named to head the American ground forces, the majority of the troops taking part would eventually be French. This led De Gaulle at one point to recommend that the French be given command of the entire southern France operation. The United States, with Wilson's concurrence, rejected the proposal, explaining that since the initial assault was to be led by Americans, it should be under their control. (In private they contended the

French would be "insufferable" if given command of United States forces.)[11] Finally it was decided that the Americans would control the planning and the operation overall, and that the French would assume tactical command (through de Lattre) of their own units once the landing phase had been completed.

There were other irritants as well. The French said they required more service troops and refused to convert their combat formations into support units, "in which duty they were poor." The Americans, though stretched themselves, had little alternative but to provide the French with numerous support personnel, including field artillery and antiaircraft units along with supply troops. As the United States official historian has noted, "The situation with respect to service units was far from satisfactory."[12]

In May, the French typically seemed impervious to previous Allied amphibious experiences and boldly set out their own invasion plan, in which they suggested that Allied forces land both east and west of Toulon. General Patch rejected the French scheme on the basis that it would scatter the landing effort and thereby reduce Allied air and naval cover along with the capacity to unload supplies. In the end, the British and Americans were able to reconcile most of their problems with the French, but not without some misgivings on both sides.

Early June was a period of great Allied victories. On the fourth, Rome was captured. On the sixth, banner headlines proclaimed, "Allies Armies Land in France . . . Great Invasion is Under Way."[13] Press censorship was eased. Detail after detail of the Normandy landing was made known to the public: the assembling of the armada, the secrecy, the anxiety, the heroism involved. In the flush of these events Anvil was not forgotten, but, for the moment, pushed aside while the west celebrated.

On the tenth, the United States Joint Chiefs arrived in

London amidst the jubilation. All things seemed possible. The French Riviera invasion was brought up, but the American and British Combined Chiefs overrode their planners and thought that other operations should also be considered.[14] On the eleventh, they agreed that a three-division amphibious assault (with one airborne division) would be the best way to support Overlord. They moved up the date from August 15 to July 25 unless Allied forces in Italy failed to reach the Pisa-Rimini line in time. They discussed using solely French troops for the operation, but ultimately decided against the idea. They said that the actual place for the landing was yet to be determined, but specified that three alternative plans besides Anvil should be worked out: one for Sète, another for the Bay of Biscay in western France, and a third for the Istrian Peninsula at the head of the Adriatic. Three days later the Combined Chiefs indicated they wanted to remain flexible, but they felt that a landing at Sète aimed to link up with an attack from the west or a direct assault against France's western coast would be most likely to help Overlord. They were not, they said, inclined to favor a landing in the Marseilles area because of the strength of the coastal defenses there and "the unprofitable line of advance up the Rhône Valley." The meaning, of course, was clear: Anvil was once again in jeopardy.

At the same time, Anvil was assailed from another quarter. On June 7, Field Marshal Sir Harold Alexander, the commander of Allied ground forces in Italy, stressed the need to follow up his recent successes and proposed pursuing the campaign into northern Italy and then moving east toward Vienna or west toward Turin and Genoa and into France. If Alexander's proposal were accepted, no troops would be removed from Italy, and hence neither Anvil nor any other amphibious operation, except in support of the Italian campaign, would be forthcoming.

At first neither the Combined Chiefs nor Field Marshal Wilson, the Mediterranean theater commander, sided with Alexander. But later Wilson changed his mind and began backing his famous field commander, who had won many laurels in the African campaigns. On the fifteenth, Generals Marshall and Arnold left London to take a look at the Mediterranean situation for themselves. It soon became obvious that their euphoria, which had resulted from Overlord, had dissipated (in part, no doubt, a result of the first "buzz" bombs being dropped on London on the thirteenth.) They were not backing *any* amphibious operation; they were once again going all-out for Anvil.

During the third week in June, Marshall in a series of meetings attempted to reason, argue, cajole, and browbeat the Mediterranean commanders (including the Americans, Clark and Eaker, who were opposed) into accepting Anvil. To the familiar arguments, he added a new one, contending that Anvil was necessary because only through southern French ports could he introduce quickly into France the thirty to forty divisions that were being readied in the United States. The Channel ports would simply not be available in time to do this. Eventually, Marshall succeeded in bringing his adversaries around (in some cases reluctantly) to his point of view. As Wilson remarked after the war:

We had conferences [for] three days. . . . We argued our case and General Marshall, in his masterly manner, argued the U.S. case. I must say, after he had finished, he convined me that . . . our case . . . wouldn't stand up. The two points that struck me as the flaws in our case—the first one was that we in the Mediterranean had no idea how Eisenhower was hampered by not having the ports, you see, and the extreme importance that Marseille would be to his future campaign against Germany. . . . Another one was that the French wouldn't play on any operations across the Adriatic, and they were pressing, you might say, to go to France. . . . Once Marshall told me that, I knew that strategically [Anvil] was the only way. We had to clear our sails and get those ports going. Alexander was visibly disappointed, because he said it was knocking the stuffing out of his offensive.[15]

In addition to Marshall, Eisenhower, as overall commander of Overlord, also became directly involved in deciding Anvil's fate. Soon after the invasion, Eisenhower indicated that additional landing craft could be shifted south since the Normandy losses had been less than anticipated. But by mid-June, the realities of a difficult campaign in northern France had overtaken his earlier optimism. Fighting across hedgerow country had proved difficult and German resistance had stiffened considerably. On the nineteenth, gale force winds started lashing the Normandy coast. By the twenty-first, the United States artificial Mulberry harbor had been put out of commission and the British harbor badly damaged. Eisenhower began to fear a stalemate, and he greatly desired the introduction of additional troops and supplies into France as quickly as possible. Thus, on the twenty-third, after considering the various possibilities, he came out strongly in favor of Anvil.[16] "Anvil," he said, "opens up another gateway into France, which if not the best in geographical location, is the best we can hope to obtain at an early date. The possession of such a gateway I consider vital." He hoped that it could take place by August 15, or by the thirtieth at the latest. However, if that proved impossible, he urged that all of the French divisions and one or two of the American ones be shipped north to help support Overlord directly. At present he declared he could not ascertain the exact number of landing craft that could be spared, but he hoped that a sufficient number of that valuable commodity could be made available to ensure Anvil on a three-divisional assault basis. With Eisenhower's assistance (the British had a saying, "What Eisenhower wants, Eisenhower gets") it looked as if the French Riviera invasion would finally be implemented.

Nevertheless, the battle for Anvil was not over. At this point Churchill once again began expressing his doubts about the operation and went so far as to call for its cancellation. On June 22, he told his Chiefs of Staff that he was "not at all attracted by the prospect of an Anvil-type operation on the south coast of France."[17] In his view, it was too far removed from Overlord to have a tactical effect, and it could not be launched until the very late date of August 15. He thought it would be far better to have Alexander continue his advance into northern Italy.

At this point the intensity of the Anvil debate reached its highest pitch. Although the British Chiefs privately expressed some reservations about the feasibility of Churchill's position, they nonetheless loyally supported their Prime Minister. On the twenty-sixth, they sent the United States Joint Chiefs a message which in effect turned down Anvil and pressed for stepping up the Italian campaign.[18] They said Anvil should revert to a threat and, using one of Eisenhower's previous arguments, advocated sending north "one or more American divisions and/or all the French divisions which General Eisenhower is capable of receiving and which our shipping resources will permit us to transport."

The next day the British received the American reply. "The proposal of the British Chiefs of Staff to abandon Anvil and to concentrate on a campaign in Italy is unacceptable."[19] The memorandum then continued: "The fact that the British and US Chiefs of Staff are apparently in complete disagreement in this matter at this particular moment when time is pressing presents a most deplorable situation. We wish you to know now, immediately, that we do not accept the statements in your answer in general with relation to the campaign in Italy as sound and as in keeping with the early termination of the war." Eisenhower also lent a hand by deciding at once to release to Wilson the twenty-four LSTs, thirty-six warships, and 416 aircraft (for the airborne lift) that the Mediterranean commander had earlier requested for Anvil.[20] The SHAEF commander made it clear that even though "all of the above . . . will entail certain sacrifices to Overlord, these will be made gladly because we are convinced of the transcendent importance of Anvil."

After another reply from the British, who continued to press for a major campaign in Italy, it was obvious that the respective Chiefs of Staff were deadlocked. Only the heads of state could resolve the issue. With Roosevelt backing Anvil, and Churchill opposing it, on the twenty-eighth exchanges between the American President and the "Former Naval Person" began to be transmitted back and forth across the Atlantic on a daily basis in the hope that they could reconcile their differences. The United States Joint Chiefs also met with the British military representatives in Washington, but the hour-long closed session produced nothing by which to solve the dispute. (In another move designed to break the impasse, General Marshall went so far as to suggest that Alexander be named to command the Anvil operation.)[21]

At the same time, Harold Macmillan, then the top British civilian representative in the Mediterranean, forwarded to the Prime Minister a memorandum which he hoped would strengthen Churchill's resolve.[22] Although somewhat out of touch with recent developments, Macmillan declared that everyone agreed Overlord should receive all possible support. But "for this purpose Armpit (to give a name to the proposed Istrian operation) is as good as Anvil—probably better." It was his opinion that the Ljubljana Gap was even more vital to Hitler than southern France, and that "Hitler will react like any organism touched in one of its most sensitive spots." Warming to his subject, Macmillan added: "Anvil is of doubtful date. . . . it is planned with less experienced commanders, with inexperienced forces [*sic*], and relies largely on the French—with all the uncertainties involved." But his final point was probably closer to the reality of the situation when he stated: "If Anvil is chosen and Armpit discarded—then do let us ensure the success of Anvil. Do not starve it, either of troops or leadership. Plan it anew, and feed it from all the experience and forces that the Mediterranean commands."

On the thirtieth, prodded by his Chiefs of Staff, Churchill reluctantly started to give way, since they all believed that "the Americans are determined to carry out Anvil and would in the final event withdraw their troops from Italy." United States leaders did not actually say they would withdraw more than their three divisions allotted for Anvil, but on July 1 Churchill picked up this last point and incorporated it into his final appeal to Roosevelt.

If you still press upon us the directive of your Chiefs of Staff to withdraw so many of your forces from the Italian campaign and leave all our hopes there dashed to the ground, His Majesty's Government, on the advice of their Chiefs of Staff, must enter a solemn protest. I need scarcely to say that we will do our best to make a success of anything that is undertaken. We shall therefore forward your directive to General Wilson as soon as you let us know that there is no hope of reconsideration by your Chiefs of Staff or by yourself.[23]

Despite Churchill's grudging and ungracious acceptance of Anvil, Roosevelt's July 2 reply was cordial but firm. "I appreciate your clear exposition of your feelings and views on this decision we are making. My Chiefs of Staff and I have given the deepest consideration to these problems and to the points you have raised. We are still convinced that the right course of action is to launch Anvil at the earliest possible date."

Roosevelt's note ended the exchange. Although Churchill remained embittered toward the operation, on the same day the Combined Chiefs directed Wilson to undertake Anvil with a launching date, if possible, of August 15. He was to prepare the invasion on a three-division assault basis, supplement it with airborne troops (strength unspecified), and altogether eventually employ ten divisions. As a final touch, in another directive the Combined Chiefs changed the code name from Anvil to Dragoon for security reasons.

During the month of June, then, Anvil had passed through various gyrations. To be sure, its subsidiary nature always made it vulnerable to outside pressures. But though threatened, it had not been canceled, and by early July looked as if it would finally be implemented. Even Churchill's stubborn opposition had failed to dislodge it. The determination of United States military leaders had apparently carried the day. In effect, Anvil had developed a life of its own.

During July, two proposals were made for airborne operations, which, while not directly related to Dragoon, still would have weakened it considerably. One of the suggestions came from General De Gaulle. Early in the month he proposed an operation, code named Caiman, which called for airlifting a French parachute regiment (located in Sicily) and supporting artillery into central France.[24] This handpicked force was to bolster the Resistance effort in the area. According to De Gaulle, General Eisenhower also accepted the idea, but when Eisenhower responded several days later, it was obvious he did not share De Gaulle's enthusiasm for the project. He said he had only agreed *in principle* to such a plan and felt that De Gaulle's motives for proposing Caiman were more political than military. After that, the Free French leader's scheme received little support.

The other proposal came from General Arnold and his air staff in Washington. Their plan envisaged preliminary bombing attacks to soften up the area around Avignon, followed by a full airborne division to capture the airfields. The paratroop forces were then to be supplemented by three infantry divisions transported in by air to secure the region.[25] The airfields were to be used by heavy bombers and other aircraft to intensify the air war against Germany and to assist in the French Riviera operation once it took place.

In a tactful reply, General Eaker on July 16 explained to Arnold that an operation of this magnitude would tie up substantial numbers of air force and infantry troops for a considerable period, thereby weakening Dragoon as well as the strategic bomber offensive. He said that while he certainly appreciated this bold "forward-looking theory for airborne operations," he and the other Mediterranean commanders had no alternative but to discourage its implementation at this late date. Arnold's plan was thus forgotten.

Dragoon seemed secure. Only Churchill did not accept this fact. He still wanted to continue a strong offensive effort in Italy. On July 6, he wrote a memo to his Chiefs of Staff: "Let them take their seven divisions—three American and four French [from Italy]. Let them monopolize all the landing craft they can reach. But let us at least have a chance to launch a decisive stroke with what is entirely British and under British command. I am not going to give way about this for anybody. Alexander is to have his campaign."[26] Nevertheless, throughout July Churchill was given little room to maneuver. The British-dominated Mediterranean command did continue to search for reinforcements to mitigate the losses in Italy, and they were able to secure two divisions—one American (the 92nd) and one Brazilian—scheduled to arrive in September and October respectively. But these two untested formations would be too late and far from sufficient to make an immediate impact on the Italian campaign.

In a last-ditch attempt, the great British wartime Prime Minister made one final try to sidetrack Dragoon. It was not the Italian campaign, but the American breakout near Saint-Lô which provided him with the opportunity. By August 4, Patton's Third Army was advancing into Brittany at a rapid rate and was expected to overrun the peninsula, including its ports, within a short time. Churchill was ecstatic. He told his Chiefs of Staff that Eisenhower now wanted the French Riviera landing canceled and the Dragoon force introduced through Brittany instead.[27] He had Wilson queried to see if the divisions being assembled in the Mediterranean could be diverted to Brittany. And he followed up by sending the President a telegram to see if he would entertain the possibility.

The American response was not slow in coming. It turned out that Eisenhower was strongly opposed to any change in plans, especially since the Breton ports had not even been captured yet. Field Marshal Wilson, who had no detailed plan for such a contingency, was also opposed. So were the American Joint Chiefs of Staff. On the sixth, with Roosevelt in the Pacific, Churchill wired Harry Hopkins, the president's trusted advisor, to try and enlist his support. In Churchill's own words, Hopkins's reply the next day was "far from comforting."[28] Hopkins, too, considered altering "the strategy now would be a great mistake." His view was shared by the President. On the eighth FDR cabled the Prime Minister: "I have consulted by telegraph with my Chiefs of Staff and am unable to agree that the resources allocated to Dragoon should be considered available for a move into France via ports on the coast of Brittany. On the contrary it is my considered opinion that Dragoon should be launched as planned at the earliest possible date and I have full confidence that it will be successful and of great assistance to Eisenhower in driving the Huns from France."

With Roosevelt's reply, Churchill reluctantly gave way. The extent of his opposition to Dragoon is well brought out in his relations with Eisenhower. He met with the Supreme Allied Commander on a number of occasions during the last days of July and early August, and in one instance he was at Ike's headquarters for six hours trying to convince him of the feasibility of a Brittany operation. Even after the President's message on the eighth Churchill was so upset that he summoned Eisenhower to 10 Downing Street and threatened to go to the King and "lay down the mantle of my high office" unless Eisenhower changed his mind. The American commander held firm, but it was not for a lack of trying on Churchill's part. The irony is that, despite his opposition, the Prime Minister had already planned a trip to Italy, and he decided to take advantage of the opportunity to witness the invasion of southern France himself. The last Churchillian hurdle had been overcome. With one week to go, Dragoon had finally been given the go-ahead to proceed as planned.

The continuing debate over Anvil's status at the highest levels had not prevented detailed planning from moving ahead. The main problem for Mediterranean staff officers during the spring and summer months was to remain flexible, so that they could take advantage of Allied actions and enemy reactions and not be tied exclusively to a single course of action. Therefore, in accordance with the wishes of the Combined Chiefs, they continued to examine a number of possible amphibious operations besides Anvil, including what to do if German forces began withdrawing from southern France. But the planners' conclusion was generally the same throughout the period: whatever the circumstances, an invasion east of Toulon still seemed to hold out the best prospect for success.

In the meantime, while General Patch scurried between North Africa and Italy (with a trip to England in between), Force 163 planners worked out a number of the details. On the assumption that Anvil would be executed in August, they decided that H-hour for the invasion would be 8:00 A.M. This would allow time for heavy air and naval bombardments prior to the assault and still permit extensive unloading throughout the daylight hours. They also kept plans in being for a two- or a three-division landing, though the latter alternative was generally favored and eventually adopted. They further drew up tentative troop lists, allocated shipping, assigned aircraft (especially for Corsica, where the major tactical air effort was being based), requisitioned supplies, and noted deficiencies. These details became the basis for a succession of Anvil plans. Thus, by July 2, when Field Marshal Wilson called for Anvil to be implemented, planning for the most part had been completed.

The final outline plan of July 29 reflected many of the modifications that had been adopted since an operation in southern France had first been suggested in August 1943. Nevertheless, it still conformed essentially to its original conception.[29] The August 15 landing was to take place along a forty-five-mile stretch of French Riviera coastline between Agay and Cavalaire-sur-Mer. Three American divisions—the 3rd, 45th and 36th Infantry (the latter replacing the 85th)—were to lead the initial assault. Two-and-one-third French divisions, including portions of an armored division, were to begin landing the next day. Reinforcements would eventually bring the French total to seven divisions, and the French forces were given the responsibility of capturing Toulon between D + 15 and D + 20 and Marseilles between D + 35

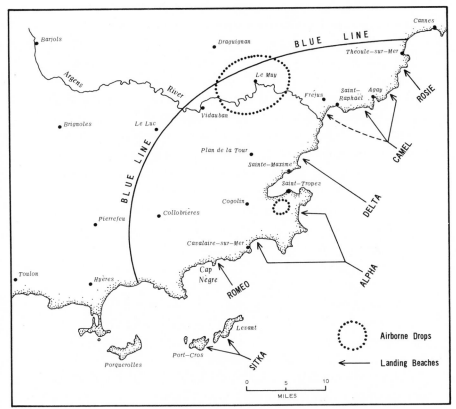

Operation Dragoon

and D + 40. Then both American and French formations were to move north toward Lyons and Vichy.

The main landing force was to be preceded the night before by a number of special units, including a large airborne contingent and French commandos and marines, who were to prevent German reinforcements from reaching the invasion beaches, and a Special Service Force of Americans and Canadians, who were to occupy two islands west of the assault area. In addition, an extensive cover plan (code named Ferdinand) was to be carried out prior to the attack. It was to include such deception measures as dummy paratroopers, misleading radio and air traffic, and misdirection of the main invasion force toward the Italian coast until the last moment, when it would swing westward for the assault.

The navy was to provide convoy and gunfire support with personnel transports being routed from ports in Italy and Algeria. Sixty-five percent of the ships were to be American, 33 percent British, and 2 percent French, Greek, and Canadian. The air contribution was to consist of large numbers of bombers, fighters, reconnaissance aircraft, and transports, which were to be flown from bases in Corsica, Sardinia, and Italy as well as from aircraft carriers at sea.

Field Marshal Wilson, whom all of the Allies, including the Americans, greatly respected for his fair-mindedness, was to exercise overall command. Once the French Riviera invasion force joined hands with Allied divisions advancing eastward across France (at some date in the future), Eisenhower was to assume control. As for the actual operation, besides General Patch directing land operations and Admiral Hewitt the naval portion, the American Brig. Gen. Gordon P. Saville, a highly regarded and efficient officer, was named to command the tactical air forces.

Even though the command structure for Dragoon was now set, in practice, of course, it was much more complicated than it appeared on paper. Normally an army group commander would direct an amphibious operation of this size. But General Patch, who was merely an army commander, was to be in charge. Only after the invasion phase had been concluded, reinforcements ashore, and a linkup with Eisenhower's forces achieved, was an army group commander to take over. This position was given to General Devers, who, as Sixth Army Group commander, would finally realize his dream of directing forces in the field. (His headquarters staff, which was established on Corsica, consisted solely of Americans, but he was fortunate in having Senator Henry Cabot Lodge, Jr., as his liaison with the French. Lodge turned out to be the perfect person to smooth over various frictions which surfaced between the United States and her French ally.)

Command complications also existed in the naval and air spheres. Although Admiral Hewitt commanded the Western Task Force, General Saville's staff naturally selected the targets for the carrier aircraft. Saville's XII Tactical Air Command also directed the fighters (mainly P-47 Thunderbolts and Spitfires) based on Corsica. But the Twelfth Air Force under Maj. Gen. Joseph Cannon controlled the medium bombers on Sardinia, and the Fifteenth Air Force under Maj. Gen. Nathan F. Twining the strategic bombers in Italy. They could be called on to help in southenn France only by order of General Eaker. While disagreements over target priorities did occur periodically, these and other difficulties were often overcome by goodwill and give-and-take among the commanders themselves. Although not having known each other previously, they got along well. The cigar-smoking Hewitt and Saville and Patch formed a competent team.

Patch also had an excellent field commander in Major General Lucian K. Truscott, Jr., who as head of VI Corps, was to lead the invasion assault. Having served in Great Brit-

ain in 1942 and a veteran of the North African, Sicilian, and
Italian amphibious operations, Truscott came to think highly
of Patch. In his memoirs Truscott recalled their meeting in
Algiers in June 1944. "He [Patch] was thin and wiry, simple
in dress and forthright in manner—obviously keenly intelligent and with a dry Scottish humor. His quick and almost
jerky speech movement gave me the impression he was ner-
vous and found some difficulty expressing himself. Our con-
versation during the evening concerned the war experiences."[30] Truscott then added, "I had no occasion to change
my views about General Patch: I came to regard him highly
as a man of outstanding integrity, a courageous and competent leader, and an unselfish comrade-in-arms."

Like Truscott, the United States divisions spearheading
the attack had a good deal of experience behind them. Truscott's old division, the 3rd, was to land in the western portion
of the lodgment on the Cavalaire-sur-Mer beaches and the
Saint-Tropez peninsula. Now under the command of Maj.
Gen. John W. "Iron Mike" O'Daniel, it had more amphibious
experience than any other division in the Mediterranean,
having participated in landings in Morocco, Sicily, and Italy.
Not far behind in experience was the 45th, the "Thunderbird" Division, which was to land in the center near Sainte-
Maxime. Originally from Oklahoma, it had helped lead the
assaults in Sicily and at Salerno, and its commander, Maj.
Gen. William W. Eagles, was also a combat veteran. The invasion zone farthest to the east near Saint-Raphaël was entrusted to the 36th Infantry Division. While the "Texas" Division had a new commander, Maj. Gen. John E. Dahlquist,
brought over from the States, it, too, was a seasoned outfit,
having participated extensively in amphibious and land operations in Italy. Dahlquist, a Minnesotan, wrote to his wife
Ruth just after having assumed command on July 10: "From

now on I am a Texan. I really am awfully lucky and I just hope to measure up to the job. It is going to be tough."[31] By this time all three divisions had been removed from the front lines in Italy and had started amphibious training, which lasted approximately three weeks, along various beaches near Naples.

The immediate French follow-up force also consisted of veteran formations. To be sure, like their American counterparts, they had suffered numerous casualties in the Italian campaign, but there was no doubt that the 1st French and 3rd Algerian Infantry divisions had proven themselves in combat. They were expected to serve with even greater distinction on French soil. The only untried formation to be immediately involved was the 1st Combat Command, whose 4,000 troops formed a portion of the 1st Armored Division.[32] But it also included a nucleus of battle-hardened troops who had served in other units. After D + 5 these French forces were to be reinforced by additional French soldiers—the 2nd Combat Command, the 9th Colonial Division, and the famous Moroccan Tabors, who, along with their mules, were noted for their exploits in mountainous terrain. Together they were to lead the attack against Toulon. Later on, the rest of the 1st Armored Division and the 2nd Moroccan, 4th Mountain, and 5th Armored divisions were to arrive in the area, bringing the French total to seven divisions plus various special forces.

Largest among the Allied special units was the Provisional Airborne Task Force. Commanded by United States Maj. Gen. Robert T. Frederick, who was known as a fearless fighter (he had reportedly been wounded at least nine times in battle), the combined paratroop and glider force included the only British soldiers to participate in Dragoon, the highly regarded, 2,000-man Independent Parachute Brigade. The task force's 9,000 troops were to capture and hold the important road junction of Le Muy, thirteen miles inland from the coast, until help arrived from the main invasion force.

Another special unit, the 1st Special Service Force, which consisted of 2,000 Americans and Canadians, was to assault the offshore islands of Port-Cros and Levant and destroy the enemy defenses there. It was considered particularly important for them to capture a coastal battery on the east end of Levant, for it overlooked the western approach of the main invasion force. These troops knew their business. Some of the Americans had scaled the cliffs at Kiska in the Aleutians and had also taken part in the Anzio operation.

Finally, nearly 1,000 French commandos were to land at night immediately west of the invasion area, secure the region, and hold off any German reinforcements until help arrived. On the right flank, sixty-seven specially trained French marines were to land in rubber rafts, and stop reinforcements which the Germans might attempt to rush toward the lodgment from the east.

Organizing Admiral Hewitt's Western Task Force for convoy and gunfire support duties required a good deal of expertise as well as plain hard work. Mounting schedules from embarkation points in Italy, Sicily, Corsica, Malta, and North Africa had to be synchronized, attack forces allocated and assembled, battle plans for gunfire coordinated between the navy and the air force. In the end, as in the case of the land forces, previous experience made these and other tasks much less formidable than would have been the case earlier in the war.

By early August, Hewitt's task force consisted of 880 ships and some 1,370 smaller vessels (mostly landing craft).[33] Included among the combat ships were five battleships (including the USS *Arkansas*, *Nevada*, and *Texas*), nine escort carriers (seven of which were British), twenty-four cruisers, 111 destroyers, and 100 minesweepers.

As in all combined operations, air power was also to play a key role in Dragoon. Tactical and coastal air formations at fourteen bases in Corsica included eighteen squadrons of P-47s, six of P-38s (on loan from the Fifteenth Strategic Air Force), twelve of Spitfires, one of night fighting Beaufighters, four of A-20 fighter bombers, twelve of B-25 Mitchells, and five equipped for reconnaissance purposes, or fifty-eight squadrons in all.[34] These were backed up by sixteen squadrons of B-26 Marauders on Sardinia and 214 carrier-based aircraft. As the time of the invasion approached, the Mediterranean air commander would increasingly call on an additional 1,271 heavy bombers, 114 medium bombers, and 437 long-range P-51 fighter escorts from the Fifteenth Air Force in Italy. This meant that, including 412 troop carrier planes, a total of 4,056 aircraft could be made available, if necessary, to support Dragoon. Even taking into account other tasks and the multitudinous problems of keeping aircraft in commission, this number (about half of the total used for Overlord) obviously represented a formidable air armada.

Long before the invasion force was being assembled, Allied aircraft had already begun the softening up process. While some of the sorties could be construed as support for Overlord, most of them were more appropriately related to the French Riviera operation. Plans for Dragoon called for the air offensive to take place in four phases.[35] During Phase 1, which was to last until five days before the invasion, bombers and fighters were to attack a variety of targets in the area, including road networks, railway bridges, military installations, ammunition dumps, and the like. Phase 2, called Operation Nutmeg, was to last from D − 5 to 3:50 A.M. on D day. It was to consist of air strikes against targets in the projected battle area as well as other targets along the coast so as not to tip off the actual locations of the attack. At 3:50 A.M. on D day all available aircraft were to concentrate on neutralizing what was left of the enemy defenses near the landing beaches. This third phase, Operation Yokum, was to end at 7:30 to allow the troops to come ashore. Once the assault units had started landing, Phase 4, Operation Ducrot, or all-out support for the Allied attacking force, was to be put into effect.

Preliminary bombing began on April 28 with a B-25 attack on Toulon. While operations in Italy kept many of the Mediterranean pilots and aircrews busy throughout May and June, they still managed to hit a variety of targets in the south of France, some as far inland as Lyons. During July the air offensive intensified, and General Eaker began to shift strategic bombers away from targets in Germany to the French Mediterranean area. On July 5, 228 B-17s and 319 B-24s from Italy bombed railway yards at Montpellier and Béziers and naval installations at Toulon. On July 11, portions of General Twining's Fifteenth Air Force returned to drop 200 tons of bombs on Toulon. The next day, 421 four-engined British Liberators hit rail yards at Miramas and Nîmes near the mouth of the Rhône along with bridges east of Toulon where the invasion was to take place. At the same time, B-25 and B-26 medium bombers, A-20 fighter bombers, and P-38, P-47, and Spitfire fighters were attacking targets all across the area.

By August 4, when the final bombing plan was issued, Allied commanders had decided to devote their primary attention for the next five days to striking enemy airfields and radar sites along with transportation and other military targets. In addition to bombing airfields around Marseilles, Toulon, and Avignon, air leaders dispatched ninety-nine heavily escorted B-26 Marauders against Bergamo-Seriate, probably the most important German air installation in Italy, and achieved good results. At the same time, American and British aircrews were bombing other targets throughout northern Italy.

Meanwhile, Allied airmen were subjecting the road and rail networks in southern France to devastating attacks. The most remarkable result was achieved on the major railway bridges spanning the Rhône from Lyons south to the Mediterranean coast. By August 9, five of the six bridges had been rendered unserviceable, and the sixth at Avignon restricted to limited use. In addition, all double track rail lines between Lyons and Avignon had been cut in two or more places. All in all, between April 28 and August 10, when the first phase ended, Mediterranean Air Force planes flew approximately 6,000 sorties and dropped 12,500 tons of bombs on southern France.

On the tenth, Operation Nutmeg, the heavy preinvasion phase, commenced. Emphasis was placed on attacking coastal gun batteries and radar stations in four general areas: west of the Rhône, Marseilles and the mouth of the Rhône, the actual landing beaches, and around Genoa in Italy. When the weather was clear, 1,000-plus sorties per day now became common. Using general purpose and fragmentation bombs, the Allies (including fifteen French squadrons) inflicted considerable damage. Overall, between August 10 and 15, the Allies flew 5,408 effective sorties, divided about equally between strategic and tactical aircraft, and dropped 7,357 tons of bombs. Of this total, only about 1,800 tons were directed against targets in the assault area, and Allied commanders believed they had succeeded in keeping the actual place of the invasion secret from the Germans. The losses during Nutmeg were astonishingly low—fifty planes, including fifteen heavy bombers, four medium bombers, twenty-nine fighters, and two patrol craft. It seemed that Air Marshal Slessor's comment that the Luftwaffe could "virtually be ignored" was being borne out by events.[36]

At the same time, French Resistance groups ably supported the Allied bombing effort. From May until July 15 they geared their sabotage activities primarily to assisting the Overlord campaign.[37] But after July 15, Field Marshal Wilson's Mediterranean command assumed control of the Resistance fighters in the south, and from that point on, most measures were undertaken to pave the way for Dragoon. Many of the Resistance targets were laid on after conferring by wireless with intelligence centers in London and Algiers. They were color-coded according to the objective to be attacked—green for rail, blue for electrical, purple for telephone and telegraph lines, and so on. The results were impressive. An indication of their effectiveness can be seen from the fact that by August 10 all secondary rail lines in the Grenoble area as well as those west of the Rhône between Limoges and Marseilles had been cut.

Assisting the Resistance units, which were controlled militarily by De Gaulle's French Forces of the Interior, were a number of special teams flown in by the Allies from the outside. From May to mid-July, Allied Special Intelligence dispatched 500 personnel along with 651 tons of war material into southern France, and from July to early September another 794 troops (including a number of Jedburgh teams consisting of one each French, American, and British officers) and 673 tons of supplies were flown in.

Just as important was the intelligence information the Resistance was sending out daily to the Allies about enemy dispositions and movements. By early August this information was coming from so many Resistance sources—mainly radio and by intelligence chains (often through Spain)—and so complete and accurate, that any German military activity was almost immediately known to the Allies. This was possible because they had achieved double, triple, and sometimes even greater coverage at key junctions along the Rhône Valley and the Mediterranean coast. Even when the Germans were able to penetrate and take over sending stations, as in the case of "Menado" near Toulon, the false information which they transmitted, while misleading to the Allies, did not lead Allied intelligence operators to reveal to the Germans the most prized information of all—the time and place of the landing.

Did the Germans ever find out when and where the invasion would take place? As of August 1, they were not sure. By the seventh, however, situation reports from Army Group G indicated that "systematic, especially heavy air attacks on the transportation links over the Rhône and Var Rivers point to a landing between these two rivers" and that "statements from agents confirm this assumption."[38] Although the information contained in these reports did not pinpoint the exact location, it had reduced the area of probability to 150 miles of Provençal coastline. It also meant that the three Wehrmacht divisions directly involved should be placed on increased alert. This occurred on the twelfth, when numerous rumors from sources within the Resistance and from the populace at large indicated that August 15, Napoleon's birthday, would be the day of attack. Additional Allied measures prior to the fifteenth, such as increased air activity, the forming up of convoys, and the actual loading of personnel at Ajaccio in Corsica, only tended to confirm, in German eyes, their earlier reports. The typical German soldier held much the same view. On the thirteenth, one of them wrote to his wife: "We will probably not have to wait very long until the invasion takes place. It is believed that the bombardments are a prelude [to the battle] as was the case in Normandy."[39]

If the Germans needed any further proof, they might

have reached a similar conclusion by examining the various news releases which were appearing in the Allied press. On the twelfth, for instance, the *New York Times* reported that nearly 1,000 American heavy bombers from Italian bases hit a 120-mile strip of fortifications along the French and Italian Riviera.[40] In the same article, the correspondent added: "Large and thinly garrisoned, this region [south of the Loire] had been increasingly vulnerable since D-day. The new wounds being punched by Allied air power in the 'underbelly' are at a point offering an avenue into Nazi-held Europe past the western wing of the Alps."

The problem was, even though the Germans knew the approximate location and the exact date of the attack, there was little they could do about it. Originally, General Blaskowitz had hoped to use both of the panzer formations he had at his disposal as a strategic reserve. But by August, one of them, the 9th Panzer Division, had been moved out. The other, the 11th Panzer, was also scheduled to be sent north. On the twelfth, however, Blaskowitz had that order rescinded, and the next day he directed that it begin moving east from Toulouse across the Rhône River toward the expected battle zone.[41] He also stopped the movement of the 338th Infantry Division out of the region and declared his intention to shift the 198th Infantry Division east along the coast so that it could be positioned near Toulon. But the possibility of receiving additional land reinforcements was slight. Field Marshal von Kluge, Commander-in-Chief West, had already reduced the number of divisions guarding France's Atlantic coast from four to two, and German formations in Italy were also stretched to the limit.

Blaskowitz and his field commander, General Wiese, head of Nineteenth Army, realized they would have to depend primarily on the eight and two-thirds divisions they had at hand. General Wiese had under him three corps, which, in turn, exercised control over six and two-thirds divisions deployed along the coast.[42] Three of them—the 716th Infantry, 198th Infantry, and 189th Reserve—were located west of the Rhône. They had only recently been brought into the region, and except for the 198th, lacked sufficient mobility to be used for offensive operations. In the center, at the mouth of the Rhône, was positioned two-thirds of the 338th Infantry Division. It had been stationed in the area for some months, but the fact that part of the division had been moved north left it in an unsettled condition.

The three divisions east of the Rhône were better equipped and each of them had approximately 12,769 troops in their ranks. (The 12,769 figure was the number the Germans used in 1944 for an infantry division to be considered at full strength.) The 244th Infantry protected the Marseilles sector. Its commander, Maj. Gen. Hans Schaefer, had been wounded on the Russian front and was a highly respected leader. The division's main components were three infantry regiments, three artillery battalions (with twenty-four 105 mm howitzers and twelve 150 mm howitzers), three anti-aircraft companies, an antitank company, and an engineering battalion. Schaefer also exercised control over eighty-eight army and naval coastal guns located in his area. One of his major problems, however, was that the 244th was a static (*bodenständig*) division and hence, immobile.

The same limitation applied to the 242d Infantry Division, which covered the coastline from Toulon east to Agay. Commanded by Maj. Gen. Johannes Bässler, its composition was similar to that of the 244th with more than 12,000 personnel, and it had a Russian and an Armenian battalion among its ranks. The 106 coastal artillery pieces controlled by Bässler included a battery (called "Big Willie") of two 340 mm guns, and their location (in front of Toulon harbor) and range (more than twenty miles) were two of the reasons the

Allies had decided to shift the invasion from the Hyères area to beaches extending east and west of Saint-Tropez. The last coastal division—the 148th Infantry—was responsible for the area from Agay to the Italian border. It had only recently been upgraded from reserve division status. As a result, Maj. Gen. Otto Fretter-Pico's division had only two instead of the usual three infantry regiments; however, it did possess the normal complement of thirty-six artillery pieces.

The most important of the two divisions Blaskowitz had in reserve was the 11th Panzer. It had suffered heavy losses on the Eastern Front early in 1944 and had only been declared ready for action again at the end of June. Among its approximately 12,000 soldiers were a number of inexperienced personnel, but it also included a cadre of veteran troops.[43] And its commander, Maj. Gen. Wend von Wietersheim, considered its state of training to be good. Its tank strength of some twenty-five Mark IVs and fifty Mark V Panthers was less than half strength, but still capable of inflicting considerable damage. The other formation in reserve—the 157th Reserve Division—had been engaging Resistance units in the mountains near Grenoble for several months. But even though it was about at full strength, it did not have enough motor vehicles to make its presence immediately felt in the invasion area.

Overall, then, the Germans had about 34,000 combat troops positioned along that portion of the coast considered most threatened. Another 170,000, including supply and administrative personnel, were stationed in the vicinity of the French Mediterranean and might be called for eventual use. Nevertheless, Blaskowitz considered his total force to be clearly insufficient to repel a determined Allied attack.

The Germany navy had continued to deteriorate during August in the face of increased Allied bombing attacks. On August 6, an air strike aimed at Toulon naval base put four of the remaining seven U-boats out of commission, leaving only one destroyer, three submarines, and approximately seventy smaller craft in the area. The navy suffered a further setback when the commander of the entire French Mediterranean sector, Vice Adm. Paul Wever, died of a heart attack on August 11.[44] His death placed an added burden on Vice Adm. Heinrich Ruhfus, the naval commander at Toulon, who had to take over temporarily Wever's duties at Aix-en-Provence until a replacement, Vice Adm. Ernst Scheurlen, arrived on August 17.

German air power was also in a weakened condition. The Allies had a fairly accurate estimate of the number of aircraft the Germans had available in southern France, and their main fear was that the Luftwaffe might decide to shift reinforcements quickly from northern France or Italy to Provence, thereby augmenting its small numbers in the region. The air unit tactically responsible for the French Mediterranean was the 2nd Air Division.[45] It had in commission about sixty-five Ju-88 bombers, thirty Messerschmitt Bf-109 and FW-190 fighters, and thirty-five reconnaissance aircraft of various types. Many of the planes, which flew from airfields at Marignane and Istres northwest of Marseilles and from Avignon and Orange farther inland, were equipped with aerial torpedoes and armor-piercing bombs for operations at sea. Also close at hand in southwestern France were fifteen unreliable He–177 and thirty Do–217 bombers and some additional fighters attached to X Air Corps. A further fifty single-engine fighters could also be brought in from Italy on short notice. This brought the total of German aircraft in the general vicinity to about 230 "ready for action," of which probably 80 percent were serviceable.

By August 15, the Allies did not expect the German units along the French Mediterranean to pose a serious deterrent to their vastly superior invasion force. Although the discrepancy between the total land forces was not great—250,000 to 210,000—the Allied troops were clearly of higher quality and better equipped than their German counterparts. Added to that, the Allies possessed a true invasion fleet and, by any standard, a huge air component, while the German navy and air force had dwindled to almost insignificant proportions. The Allies even had indications through Ultra intelligence that their northerly advance might be much more rapid than they had originally envisaged.[46]

Nonetheless, they were well aware that an amphibious operation is especially vulnerable during its initial stages, that the Germans would probably hold on tenaciously to Toulon and Marseilles, and that the mountainous terrain inland could prove exceedingly difficult to traverse. They had engaged the Wehrmacht soldier enough times to realize that an easy victory was not assured.

4

The Invasion

THE INVASION was to take place along a forty-five-mile stretch of coastline between the small resort villages of Cavalaire-sur-Mer and Agay. In between there were no towns of any great size. Saint-Tropez, which sits on a peninsula jutting out into the sea, had some harbor facilities, but was considered too well defended to be attacked frontally. Fréjus and Saint-Raphaël, in the eastern portion of the projected battle zone, normally in peacetime bustling with tourist activity at this time of year, lay relatively deserted, in their own ways casualties of the war.

The shoreline along this portion of the French Riviera is spectacularly beautiful, the beaches narrow—seldom more than fifty yards wide—the view from the pine-covered hillsides breathtaking. Behind the sand or shingle beaches, stretching almost the entire length of the invasion area, is a series of hills known as the Monts des Maures, which reach heights of 1,000 to 1,500 feet. Dividing the Monts des Maures and the dark red cliffs of the Estérel, at the eastern end of the projected lodgment, is the valley of the Argens River. The Argens, which flows in an easterly direction and

empties into the Mediterranean west of Saint-Raphaël, sepa-
rates the heights along the coast from the Provence Alps further inland, and it, along with some narrow passages
through the Monts des Maures, forms several natural corri-
dors into the interior.

To the west lay the major military objectives of the operation—the naval base at Toulon, the port of Marseilles, the
Rhône River valley leading northward into central France.
Capturing them was most feasible by land. (The sea approaches had been ruled out because of the formidable German coastal batteries in front of Toulon and Marseilles.) For
transport, the Allies expected to rely primarily on three main
highways in the region. Highway 7 was a two lane, macadam
road which ran west from Fréjus to Aix-en-Provence and
then on to Avignon and up the Rhône. Highway 97 branched
off Highway 7 near Le Luc and extended southwest into
Toulon. It was two lane and considered capable of carrying
all types of military traffic. The same could not be said of
Highway 98, which generally followed along the coast, and
which could be easily blocked. An additional transport possibility was a double-track railway which ran several miles inland from the coast, with spur lines connecting it to the various seaside resorts.

The weather along this stretch of coastline in August is
usually ideal—warm, sometimes hot days, relatively cool
nights (at least near the coast) with fresh sea breezes. There
are no swollen rivers, no extreme tides, no gusty winds (the
dreaded *mistrals*) out of the Alps with which to contend at
this time of the year. It was not only the perfect time and
place for a holiday; it was also the perfect time for an amphibious invasion.

The Allies set Dragoon in motion on August 9.[1] During
the next four days the main assault force, consisting pri-

marily of the 3rd, 45th, and 36th United States divisions, loaded into troop transports, Landing Craft Infantry (LCIs), and Landing Craft Tanks (LCTs) and sailed from the Naples area. Their battleship, cruiser, and destroyer escorts joined them at sea. At about the same time, the two and one-third French follow-up divisions and their equipment started departing from Taranto and Brindisi in southern Italy and from Oran in Algeria. On the twelfth, the aircraft carrier task force of nine carriers, four cruisers, and thirteen destroyers put out to sea from Malta. Fighter aircraft, primarily from Mediterranean Coastal Air Command, provided additional cover for the convoys as they headed toward their final rendezvous point west of Corsica.

The voyage was uneventful. For three days and three nights the convoys (except for those from North Africa) passed through the straits between Sardinia and Corsica. Briefings were held, maps passed out and studied. A nonchalant, almost blasé attitude seemed to be the dominant mood. General Truscott, who was to command the main assault force, noted that the heat aboard ship was oppressive, but that otherwise everything was quiet.[2] Reporter Will Lang, writing about the invasion for *Life*, recorded: "When a small radio was tuned in to 'Axis Sally,' . . . and she boasted that the Germans knew all about the coming invasion of Southern France, the soldiers kept on playing cards or talking quietly. Finally the ship's chaplain couldn't stand it any longer. 'This bunch of men are awfully unexcited,' he complained. 'I just had a normal crowd at services this morning. On the way across the Channel from England almost everybody turned out.'"[3] General Dahlquist, head of the 36th Division and participating in his first amphibious attack, did not seem overly anxious either. On the fourteenth he wrote to his wife, Ruth: "An amphibious operation is the most complicated of all military operations. . . . For good or for bad, however, my part is done until tomorrow morning. We are in the hands of the Navy until we get ashore."[4]

And Admiral Hewitt's Western Task Force was performing its duties in exemplary fashion. Everything was running as smoothly as could be expected. More than 100,000 sailors were making sure that loading schedules were being met, convoys assembled, and escorts provided. Moreover, a number of the 880 United States, British, French, and Greek ships were also to furnish gunfire support for the troops as they moved ashore. Nine aircraft carriers (seven British and two American), each with twenty-four aircraft on deck, were to provide additional naval firepower. All in all, it was truly an impressive armada which bore down on the French Riviera coast.

The main invasion force was to assault three major beach areas: Alpha on the left, Delta in the center, and Camel on the right. Although their individual missions varied, the three American divisions were to overcome enemy resistance on their respective beaches and advance inland approximately twenty miles to an imaginary (except on the battle maps) "blue line" running in an arc from near Saint-Honoré in the west to Théoule-sur-Mer in the east. Once the forces reached this line, they were to receive further orders for the next phase of the operation.

The much-publicized and highly decorated United States 3rd, "Iron Mike" O'Daniel's "Old Guard" division, was to lead the attack in the Alpha sector. Like the other two lead divisions, the 3rd had a tank and a tank destroyer battalion added to its normal complement, thus raising its combat strength to 16,000 troops.[5] This number, plus approximately 14,000 service troops, brought the 3rd Division total to more than 30,000 personnel who would eventually come ashore across Alpha's beaches. For combat purposes, the 3rd was

Gen. Jacob L. Devers, deputy commander of the Mediterranean Theater at the time of the Anvil/Dragoon operation, in July 1945. (Photograph courtesy of United States Army, SC 209782)

Lt. Gen. Alexander M. Patch, Jr., the driving force in the planning of the Anvil/Dragoon operation, and commanding general, Seventh Army, wearing his famous violet scarf. (Photograph courtesy of United States Army, SC 196341)

Gen. Johannes Blaskowitz, as commander of German Army Task Force G, assumed control of all southern France from the Atlantic to the Italian border. (Photograph courtesy of United States National Archives)

Left to right: *Lt. Gen. Lucian K. Truscott, Jr., commander of United States VI Corps, talking with Maj. Gen. John W. O'Daniel, his 3rd Division commander. (Photograph courtesy of United States Army, SC 195814)*

Soldiers of the United States 45th Division, with jeeps, trucks, and 155 mm howitzers, board LSTs near Naples in preparation for the invasion. (Photograph courtesy of United States Army, SC 193362)

A Fifteenth Air Force B-24 flies over Sète after a bombing run on August 12. (Photograph courtesy of United States Air Force, 59849AC)

Allied convoys en route to southern France. (Photograph courtesy of United States Army, SC 193193)

The American cruiser Brooklyn opens fire on the Mediterranean coast with French warship Emile Bertin in background. (Photograph courtesy of United States National Archives, 245613)

The jumpmaster (standing) gives final instructions to United States paratroopers just before reaching their drop zone in southern France. (Photograph courtesy of United States Air Force, 53420)

American paratroopers of the 1st Airborne Task Force move along a dusty road near Le Muy. (Photograph courtesy of United States Army, SC 377602)

Infantry troops of the 45th Division come ashore near Sainte-Maxime on D day. (Photograph courtesy of United States Army, SC 193146)

American assault troops come ashore and pour through a breach blasted in an eight-foot-high concrete and steel German defense wall on Delta beach on invasion day. (Photograph courtesy of United States Army, SC 193147)

Lieutenant General Patch congratulates Sgt. James P. Connor after the latter received the Medal of Honor. Sergeant Connor, though wounded three times, heroically led a platoon after its leaders were killed in the invasion-day assault against Cape Cavalaire. Major General O'Daniel looks on. (Photograph courtesy of United States Army, SC 436612)

Troops of the 15th Infantry Regiment, 3rd Division, await orders to advance inland after landing on the Alpha beaches. (Photograph courtesy of United States Army, SC 270615)

United States assault troops push forward against light opposition. (Photograph courtesy of United States National Archives, 59469)

A tank destroyer is off-loaded onto an LCT to be carried to the beach near Saint-Tropez. (Photograph courtesy of United States Army, SC 193350)

Antiaircraft half-tracks being unloaded off an LCT in the 3rd Division (Red beach) area. (Photograph courtesy of United States Army, SC 192870)

Vice Adm. H. Kent Hewitt, head of the Eighth Fleet and commander of the Anvil/Dragoon naval task force, talking with a beachmaster as unloading of equipment proceeds apace on D + 1. (Photograph courtesy of United States National Archives, 242133)

Famous French Tabors, fierce Moroccan fighters, move toward the front lines with their mules. (Photograph courtesy of United States National Archives, 243580)

United States 45th Division soldiers and a tank move ahead west of Draguig-nan. (Photograph courtesy of United States Army, SC 271435)

An American 3rd Division soldier walks past a picture of the Fuehrer in the streets of Brignoles. (Photograph courtesy of United States Army, SC 270617)

French Resistance fighters deal with a female collaborator in Toulon. (Photograph courtesy of United States National Archives, 243583)

Wounded being carried along the beach prior to being loaded into LSTs in the 3rd Division (Red beach) sector. (Photograph courtesy of United States Army, SC 192868)

French soldiers parade down Boulevard de Strasbourg in celebration of the liberation of Toulon. (Photograph courtesy of United States Army, SC 193525–S)

French troops engaged in house-to-house fighting in Marseilles, storming the heights where the basilica of La Notre Dame de la Garde is located. The soldier in the foreground has a rifle rigged as a grenade launcher. (Photograph courtesy of United States Army, SC 193522–S)

Effects of German demolitions in the harbor at Marseilles. (Photograph courtesy of United States Army, SC 193878)

"Big Willie," the 340 mm guns which helped guard the harbor at Toulon. A 76 mm gun is mounted on the top of the turret. (Photograph courtesy of United States Army, SC 195554)

An American tank rolls past destroyed German vehicles on Highway 7 north of Montélimar. (Photograph courtesy of United States Army, SC 193797)

Allied soldiers and French partisans clear out German snipers across the Rhône River in Lyons. (Photograph courtesy of United States Army, SC 193871)

Riding on a tank, American infantrymen move past an abandoned German vehicle in pursuit of its former operators. (Photograph courtesy of United States Army, SC 193137)

Soldiers of Company A, 30th Infantry Regiment, 3rd Division, cross the Doubs River in Besançon. (Photograph courtesy of United States Army, SC 270623)

A flour manufacturer and his eleven-year-old daughter, in Luxeuil, give a bottle of wine to T.Sgt. Joe Tradenick of the 141st Infantry Regiment, 36th Division, as he marches through the town. (Photograph courtesy of United States Army, SC 195295)

Lieutenant General Devers (second from left) *with* (left to right) *French Generals Jean de Lattre de Tassigny, Marie Emile Béthouart, and Goislard de Monsabert at the* Lion of Belfort *(Franco-Prussian War memorial), Belfort, France, November 1944. At the time of the Riviera invasion, de Lattre was head of French Army B (changed to First French Army on September 15), de Monsabert head of the 3rd Algerian Division (became head of I Corps on September 2), and Béthouart was in Italy (became head of II Corps on September 2). (Photograph courtesy of United States Army, SC 198128)*

divided into three regimental combat teams, each numbering about 5,500 troops. Each of them had a proportion of
sixty tanks (fifty-four of which were mediums) and sixty antitank guns attached. Their firepower was further augmented by twelve additional 155 mm guns which had been
added to the division's usual allotment of fifty-four 105 mm
and twelve 155 mm howitzers.

At 8:00 A.M., one of the combat teams was to land at Cavalaire Bay on the left of the Alpha zone (code named Alpha
Red). At the same time another combat team was to disembark on the right in the middle of the Saint-Tropez peninsula
(Alpha Yellow). Once they had established a beachhead, a
third follow-up regiment was to come ashore that same day
and take its place beside the other two 3rd Division regiments.

The 45th "Thunderbird" Division, which was to land on
the Delta beaches in the center, was similar in composition to
the 3rd—three regimental combat teams; added firepower
in the form of tanks, mobile antitank guns, and additional
artillery pieces; 16,000 combat soldiers, 30,000 troops in all.[6]
Its commander, Gen. William Eagles, though not as colorful
as General O'Daniel, was a seasoned and competent leader
nonetheless.

Allied planners had decided not to risk having the 45th
attack at the head of the Gulf of Saint-Tropez because of
possible flanking fire on both sides. Instead two of the combat teams were to assault 5,000 yards of beach east of Sainte-
Maxime (Delta Red, Green, Yellow, and Blue) and then fan
out along the coast and into the interior. As was the case with
the 3rd Division, a third regiment was to reinforce the other
two as soon as possible, preferably during the morning
hours.

Though similar in make-up to the other two divisions, the
36th "Texas" Division, with its golden T shoulder patch,

faced a different situation on the Camel beaches to the right.[7] One of the beaches, west of Saint-Raphaël (Camel Red) was considered vital, for it lay near the mouth of the Argens River and thus provided a convenient corridor for troops to advance inland between the coastal hills. But the beach was well defended with underwater mines as well as an array of coastal artillery guns. Therefore, two of General Dahlquist's combat teams were to land farther east at two smaller beaches (Camel Green and Camel Blue) in the morning. While one of the combat teams followed the coast northeast toward Cannes, the other was to move west into Saint-Raphaël and put pressure on German forces protecting Camel Red beach. This move, combined with a large-scale air and naval bombardment, was to allow a third regiment to come ashore at Camel Red beach in the afternoon, capture Fréjus that evening, and then move quickly inland along the Argens River. If all went well, the Allies hoped to land some 50 to 60,000 soldiers and 6,500 vehicles on all of the beaches during the first day.

The German division deployed in the invasion area was the 242nd. Because the Germans were not sure of the exact location of the attack, the division commander had to space his 12,000 troops along the entire coastline from Toulon to Agay, with a considerable proportion of them (including the naval forces) stationed at Toulon. The division went on alert on August 12, but it was thought to be little more than a stopgap against the Allied invaders.

Since their naval and air forces were of negligible value, the Germans hoped that the 11th Panzer could beat back the invader in a decisive counterattack. General Wietersheim's division had 12,000 troops and was ordered to begin moving east from the Toulouse area on the thirteenth. But it experienced difficulties from the start.[8] As a result of Allied air superiority, the division was supposed to travel only at night;

however, this was soon abandoned because of the long distances involved. Still movement was slow, and the line of advance had to be camouflaged so that the tank units and other formations could move from one point of cover to another without being detected. This problem was compounded by the fact that French Resistance fighters controlled the area north of the highway, and any "stringing out" of the columns often led to an ambush of individual vehicles.

Even when portions of the division reached the Rhône near Avignon, its troubles were not over. There was only one bridge which was still usable, and it was being subjected to constant air attacks. Consequently, although some of the tanks were able to cross the bridge at night, German engineering teams had to ferry many of them across the river. This process was only beginning on the fifteenth, the day of the invasion. The 11th Panzer was therefore in no position to meet the Allies as they began streaming ashore some 100 miles to the east.

Overall, the Allied invasion armada was indeed impressive—60,000 troops for the initial onrush, 250,000 in all. These were backed up by 880 naval vessels and 4,056 aircraft. The forces the Germans could muster were extremely meager in comparison. With the 11th Panzer unable to move east of the Rhône rapidly enough, the Wehrmacht had only approximately 6,000 combat personnel located in the invasion sector. While the total number of troops in southern France was more substantial—210,000, they could only be of use later on. And by the fifteenth, the German naval and air fleets had also been reduced to almost insignificant proportions; only seventy-five ships and 180 aircraft were located in the immediate area. This was hardly a force with which to repel a battle-hardened, well-equipped enemy.

Why then did the Germans hold on and not pull back to more defensible positions? The answer can only be surmised, for the German records are unclear on this point. Certainly, there were good reasons why they might withdraw. Naval and air superiority, vital for an amphibious attack, were clearly in the hands of the Allies. German coastal defenses, while better (especially around Toulon and Marseilles), were still not formidable enough to withstand a determined assault. In addition, the rapid advance of Eisenhower's armies across central France had placed Wehrmacht forces throughout the area in jeopardy. And now, with the French Riviera invasion in the offing, they were left with only two realistic alternatives: either withdraw or face the possibility of being cut off and captured. At the time of the Normandy breakout in late July, the Armed Forces High Command had even broached the possibility of ordering a retreat, but had decided against it for the time being. In similar instances, historians have often fallen back on Hitler's "no retreat, hold to the last man" orders as the probable explanation, but there is no indication in this case that he intervened.

Not surprisingly, the most plausible reason for the Germans not pulling back seems to be inertia. Having decided for many months to defend the coast, and with their present attention directly mainly toward trying to extricate themselves from disastrous situations on both the eastern and western fronts, the Armed Forces and Army High commands preferred to let events in southern France take their course. Despite entreaties from the commanders on the spot to the contrary, they decided not to take any drastic steps, such as a withdrawal, until an invasion had actually taken place.

Meanwhile, the Allies' invasion convoys were moving toward the target area. Originally they set a course toward Genoa in the hope of confusing the Germans, but then altered course to position themselves in front of the Provençal coast. Various special units, which were to ease the way for the main assault forces, were the first to move into action.

At 10:00 P.M. on the night of the fourteenth, the 1st Special Service Force, with 2,000 United States and Canadian commandos, started climbing over the sides of their transports and into ten-man rubber assault craft.[9] Their mission was to attack the offshore islands of Levant and Port-Cros, to the west of the Alpha beaches, and eliminate any enemy resistance there. Allied planners considered it especially important for them to seize quickly a battery of 164 mm guns located on the the east end of Levant so that it could not disrupt the main landing at Cavalaire Bay.

The specially trained 1st Special Service Force, called Sitka Force, landed unopposed a little after midnight. They proceeded to scale a series of cliffs, many forty to fifty feet high, and moved to assembly areas inland. By 9:30 initial German resistance (there were about 850 troops on the islands) had been overcome. When the commandos reached the artillery guns, they found them to be wooden dummies. By late evening of the fifteenth all opposition on Levant had ceased. On Port-Cros, only a pocket of Germans held out in an old fort at the western end of the island. While playing no part in the main battle, they refused to surrender until the seventeenth.

At the same time, approximately 1,000 French commandos, the first soldiers to land on southern French soil, started securing the left flank west of Cavalaire Bay. Romeo Force, as it was known, experienced some difficulties in the landings—some of them being put ashore on the wrong beaches, but they were able to accomplish their tasks by destroying the enemy defenses on Cap Nègre, establishing a road block on the coastal highway, and then capturing high ground two miles to the north. Having suffered only light casualties, they contacted elements of the 3rd Division moving west from Alpha Red beach early on the first afternoon.

On the eastern flank, near Théoule-sur-Mer, a demolition party of sixty-seven French marines, or Rosie Force, was not so fortunate. As the men disembarked from their rubber assault craft, they ran into barbed wire and antipersonnel mines. The resulting explosions alerted the enemy, who began firing at the marines with deadly effect. By the time they made contact with the United States 36th Division the next day, only about thirty survivors were left, and many of them were wounded. (They were also not helped by the fact that several Allied fighter planes strafed their positions early on D day.)

The largest special force, Rugby Force, was to be airdropped into three zones inland close to the road and rail junction of Le Muy.[10] For the initial drop, more than half of the 9,000 airborne troops were loaded into 412 C–47 troop carrier aircraft near Rome. News reporter Newbold Noyes, Jr., described the scene as follows: "The British paratroopers with which I flew were magnificent. At the take-off in Italy, as our ship shuddered for a second at the top of the runway before hurtling into the darkness, one pink-faced boy, grotesque in his bulky paraphernalia, threw back his head and shouted above the roar of the motors: 'Look out, Jerry, here we come!'"[11] Preceding the troop carrier force were Pathfinder aircraft, and they, along with beacon ships, helped guide the C–47s toward their drop zones. The Le Muy area was shrouded in fog, however, and the drop had to be executed blind. Even so, between 4:30 and 5:15 A.M., approximately 85 percent of the troops landed in their proper sectors. They immediately began to assemble and cleared the area against only token resistance.

Only two groups of planes completely missed their targets. About twenty-five aircraft dropped American and British paratroopers near Fayence, fifteen miles north of Le Muy. Some of the men made their way back to Allied lines, but others had to hold out, with partisan assistance, until help arrived on the nineteenth. In the other instance, twenty-nine aircraft lost their way in the fog and dropped most of their troops in a pine forest three miles south of Saint-Tropez, or more than twenty miles from the intended landing zone. Unfortunately, a few of the parachutists landed in the sea, but most of them managed to assemble during the early morning hours. They then proceeded to put five airlifted artillery pieces into operation and captured a number of enemy batteries and troops before being led by Resistance fighters into Saint-Tropez itself. At the time forward elements of the 3rd Division made contact with the airborne force, they were in the process of reducing the old Citadel, the last German strongpoint in the town.

For the main force near Le Muy, seventy-one gliders began to bring in reinforcements at 9:20 A.M. A much larger contingent of 332 gliders arrived at seven o'clock that evening, and by the end of the day 9,000 airborne personnel, 221 jeeps, and 213 artillery pieces had been landed at a cost of 434 killed (including 52 British) and 292 injured. Although German soldiers stubbornly held out in the town of Le Muy until the next day, and there were other problems, such as dropping supplies from too high an altitude, causing them to drift too far from the drop zone, or at too fast a speed to reach the ground undamaged, in general the airborne drop proved to be a highly successful undertaking.

Not all of the preinvasion phase consisted of special units in action. Numerous diversionary activities, code named Ferdinand, were also taking place on the night of August 14–15.[12] Besides increased radio traffic, a group of ships and aircraft simulated a landing (rather halfheartedly because of the heavy mist and radar failures) west of the invasion area between Marseilles and Toulon. Some of the aircraft did manage, however, to drop 500 dummy paratroopers rigged with demolition charges northwest of Toulon. While the Germans soon discovered the ruse, it did cause those responsible for that stretch of the coast some anxious moments. An eastern diversion, consisting mainly of British ships, including motor launches, also simulated a landing between Cannes and Nice, but it had little effect on the enemy.

The drama of the invasion continued to unfold during the predawn hours. Three important operations had to be carried out before the main landings took place: aerial bombing, a naval bombardment, and minesweeping activities.[13] Despite the heavy fog which began to form after midnight, the winds were light and variable with calm seas.

The fog affected the bombers most. The air operation, called Yokum, started several hours later than scheduled at 5:50 A.M. Using H_2X radar and Norden bombsights "to see through the cloud cover," twelve groups of escorted heavy bombers (mostly B–17s) and two wings of medium bombers backed up by all of the resources of the XII Tactical Air Command on Corsica attempted to saturate the assault beaches with 1,000 pounds of explosives for every ten yards of beach. Their efforts were partially successful, though one-third of the 959 sorties had to abort because of the severe ground fog and haze over the target areas. By 7:30, when Yokum ceased to allow the invasion force to come ashore, they had dropped 774 tons of explosives. The results showed that the Alpha beaches in particular had been well hit, while the results on the Delta and Camel beaches to the north and east were more spotty. But even in the latter case 163 B–25s managed to bomb the northern portion of Camel Red beach with good coverage.

Overlapping naval gunfire commenced just after 6:00 A.M. The fire-support forces, which aimed at known artillery batteries and strongpoints, were formidable. Off the Alpha beaches, the Allies had positioned one battleship (HMS *Ramillies* with its fifteen-inch guns), six cruisers, and six destroyers. Off Delta, two battleships (the USS *Nevada* and USS *Texas* with fourteen-inch guns), three cruisers, and eleven destroyers; and off Camel, one battleship (the USS *Arkansas*), six cruisers, and eleven destroyers. They, too, stopped firing at 7:30, but not before they had hurled 15,900 shells against the enemy's defenses.

Just before dawn, the troops of the 3rd, 45th, and 36th divisions began climbing down from their transports into hundreds of landing craft. The assault boats assembled into waves and pushed through designated paths between the fire-support ships and headed toward the French Riviera shore. The men crouched low, anticipating the command to assault the smoking beaches.

Regular- and shallow-water minesweepers went ahead and cleared 100-yard lanes to within 500 yards of shore (100 yards in the case of Alpha). Eighteen radio-operated drone boats, loaded with explosives and designed to blow up on impact with underwater mines, were used to extend the lanes even farther toward the beaches. (Fifteen of them detonated properly, but one got out of control, turned back toward the fleet, and damaged an Allied submarine chaser.) Small craft served as markers along the swept lanes. Landing craft carrying rockets, tanks, and antiaircraft guns gave additional support to the assault boats as they headed for shore.

The flagship USS *Catoctin* began moving from the Alpha beaches to off Saint-Tropez, where Admiral Hewitt, the head of the Western Task Force, directed the action from the bridge. Beside him was General Patch, the overall ground commander once the troops were ashore. Nearby was General Truscott, VI Corps commander, who was responsible for the main assault phase of the operation.

A late edition of the August 15 *New York Times* inserted into its coverage of the European war a lead paragraph which read, "American, British, and French troops are landing on the southern coast of France, a special communique from Allied headquarters in Italy announced today."[14] With this inconspicuous beginning, Operation Dragoon was finally underway.

The landing beach farthest west, Alpha Red, lay at the head of Cavalaire Bay.[15] In front of the sand beach the Germans had placed a row of concrete tetrahedrons, and mines and barbed wire were strung out along the shore. Behind the beach was a narrow belt of pine-covered dunes with artillery casemates, pillboxes, and machine gun nests interspersed among them. Immediately southwest of the beach was the village of Cavalaire-sur-Mer. On the high ground surrounding the town were positioned some light antiaircraft guns and medium artillery batteries. From Cavalaire-sur-Mer, the coastline extended south to a point called Cap Cavalaire, which was also well defended. To the right of the invasion area lay cultivated fields.

The 7th Regimental Combat Team of the 3rd Division began assaulting Alpha Red beach on schedule at 8:00 A.M. The first wave was met by only scattered and largely ineffectual artillery, mortar, machine gun, and small-arms fire. The second wave was not so fortunate and was pinned down for a time by heavy enemy fire before being able to move off the beaches. A few minutes later a landing craft in the third wave blew up when it struck one of the tetrahedrons which had a teller mine attached. Eleven soldiers were killed and others injured. Nevertheless, resistance was generally light, and only fifty minutes after the first wave had landed, the Americans fired a violet signal flare into the air to indicate that the beach defenses had been neutralized and that additional forces and supplies could now be brought ashore in relative safety.

Some of the troops had been formed into battle patrols of 155 men each. Their mission was to attack and destroy the enemy gun emplacements on the left flank. One of the patrols experienced some of the hardest fighting the 3rd Davision was to face that day. The European theater history reconstructs the action in vivid detail.

This patrol's special mission was to proceed about 2,000 yards westward from the landing point to Cavalaire-sur-Mer, to clean out the town and the peninsula on which it is situated. This point of land gave the enemy a field of flanking fire and artillery observation on boats coming in to shore. As the troops turned left toward the town, they ran into minefields.

Two warnings were shouted; but at the moment 2 Lt John J. Creigh, leader of the first platoon, hit the wire of a hanging mine. He was torn to bits by the explosion; and Sgt James P. Connor, platoon guide, who had tried to halt the officer, was blown ten feet away by the concussion and wounded on the left side of his neck by fragmentation. Ignoring his bleeding wound Sgt Connor helped organize the men and move them through the minefield between the road and the sea. The Germans were spraying 20-mm flak along the road which snipers also covered by fire.

The patrol pushed forward to the road bridge just east of Cavalaire-sur-Mer. An enemy rifleman jumped up from the roadside about ten feet in front of the sergeant, who shot and killed the German without losing stride. On the other side of the bridge near a group of houses a heavy concentration of mortar fire came in. Snipers were also taking pot shots at the advancing troops. About 75 yards west of the bridge a German sniper who wounded one member of the patrol was killed by Sgt Connor. Another sniper shot killed the acting platoon leader, and Sgt Connor took over the job.

The men were anxious to take any available cover to escape the mortar fire. The new platoon leader told them to get the hell out of there and on forward, that the fire was coming from Objective P (the point at Cavalaire), that by going forward they wouldn't be hit. By this time the platoon had been reduced to about 20 men from the original 36.

As the patrol started forward a machine gun nearby opened up, but one of the men silenced this enemy gunner with a burst from his BAR. One of them shot Sgt Connor in the left shoulder. Sgt Herman F. Nevers, first squad leader, tore Sgt Connor's shirt loose, saw that he had a nasty wound and urged him to get medical attention. He refused and immediately directed the men in a flanking movement to clean out the snipers. . . .

They plunged on, through groups of buildings and lightly wooded areas, up the Cavalaire side of the point, out of mortar fire and into machine gun, rifle, and rifle grenade fire. A German suddenly came up out of a hole in front of the leaders and fired. Sgt Connor was hit in the leg and fell to the ground. Sgt Nevers fired over him and killed the German.

Sgt Connor could not stand on his leg. . . . Two other wounded men stayed with Sgt Connor, while the rest of the platoon did a right and left hook about the houses in front of them, killing three or four and capturing about 40 of the enemy. . . .

Without further serious opposition they continued to the tip of the peninsula, joining the other two platoons of the battle patrol on their right flank.[16]

The platoon had suffered about 20 casualties, but by 11:00 A.M., Cap Cavalaire was secure in American hands.

The main force of the 7th Regiment moved off in two directions. One battalion headed north and west following a coastal road. By 1:30 it had advanced five miles and had made contact with the French commandos who had landed the night before near Cap Nègre. During the rest of the day, the Americans, now two battalions strong, continued in column along the coastal road and Highway 98, farther inland.

At 11:00 P.M., however, a motorized patrol ran into an enemy roadblock west of Cap Nègre, and it had to wait until the next morning to attack the strongpoint.

The other battalion of the 7th Regiment advanced into the interior from Cavalaire Bay against light resistance. After reaching high ground, they were relieved in the afternoon by the 30th Regiment, which had landed after 9:00 A.M. as the follow-up force. While the 7th Regiment battalion moved west to rejoin its group, the 30th continued to push north and captured the towns of Cogolin, on Highway 98, and Grimaud late in the day. At nine that evening one of its patrols contacted elements of the 45th Division, which were advancing southwest from their Delta landing zone. The 30th was approximately eight miles from its starting point.

The third regiment in General O'Daniel's division, the 15th, landed at Pampelonne Bay in the middle of the Saint-Tropez peninsula. Code named Alpha Yellow, it was the largest beach in the entire invasion zone. The soft sand beach had such a steep gradient that it was suitable only for small landing craft, and in the middle of the beach was a wooded slope which tended to divide the area in two. The Germans had piled some stakes about 150 feet out into the water, had placed barbed wire and mines along the beach, and had positioned two coastal batteries and some pillboxes a little farther inland. They had also blocked the narrow beach exits with mines, wire, and debris.

The 15th Regiment's landing craft began to beach at 8:02. Because of the effectiveness of the air and naval bombardment earlier that morning, enemy resistance consisted mainly of small-arms fire. The minefields also presented few difficulties, for the French Resistance and civilians the night before had marked the locations of many of the mines and had removed others. Forty minutes after the first wave had touched down, the American troops started moving inland.

While two battalions began to clear the peninsula to the north and south, the third battalion landed in reserve and advanced northeast. Early in the afternoon they overran some hills southwest of Saint-Tropez and moved into the town. American paratroopers and members of the French Resistance were already there, and the battalion spent the rest of the afternoon assisting in final liberation of this famous coastal resort. By the end of the day, German resistance on the peninsula had ceased, and the 15th started west to join General O'Daniel's other two regiments.

The Delta beaches in the center of the invasion area were similar topographically to those at Alpha. Located on Bougnon Bay northeast of Sainte-Maxime, the 5,000-yard sand and shingle beach possessed only one natural vehicle exit, on the right where the small Garonette River empties into the sea. Behind the shoreline was a line of dunes, a coastal road and railroad, and a series of steep, pine-covered slopes which eventually leveled off toward the west into cultivated fields. The beach defenses were light except for some beach mines, a few mortars, and a concrete seawall which extended some distance on the left side of the beach and acted as an antitank deterrent. Several minutes after 8:00 A.M., the 45th landed four battalions abreast. They were met by only scattered fire since the preliminary bombardment had virtually wiped out the beach defenses. One of the few problems came about in breaching the six-foot-high, four-foot-wide seawall. Demolition charges for the mine clearing company had been placed on an amphibious tank, but the tank had sunk before it could reach shore. However, "under the direction of Pvt. Walter E. Ahrens, several of the engineers secured demolitions from the tank and put them in place. A twelve-foot gap was blown in the wall. Men, tanks, and vehicles poured through." [17] By nine o'clock seven waves had landed, and the beach was secure.

The 157th Regimental Combat Team advanced on the left, the 180th on the right. One battalion of the 157th by-passed the town of Sainte-Maxime and followed west along the Gulf of Saint-Tropez coastline. At nine that evening one of its patrols made contact with the 3rd Division. Already engineering teams were beginning to construct an airstrip near the coast.

Another battalion of the 157th swung left into Sainte-Maxime. Shortly after noon they ran into small-arms and machine-gun fire and had to use grenades in house-to-house fighting. By midafternoon, only two points of resistance remained—at the Hotel du Nord and along a quay east of town, which had a 37- and a 75-mm gun placed in pillboxes. By 5:00 P.M. these strongpoints had been reduced, and Sainte-Maxime was completely taken over.

The third battalion, followed by the 179th Regiment which had landed in reserve, pressed northwest against only token opposition. By sunset they had advanced seven miles and had reached the crossroads town of Plan de la Tour. After dark, a motorized patrol was sent toward Vidauban, which lies astride Highway 7, more than fifteen miles inland from the coast.

The other regiment of the "Thunderbird" Division, the 180th, assaulted the Delta beaches on the right. One battalion took high ground to the northwest and began moving into the interior. Another battalion also advanced inland toward the Argens River, and the third fanned out along the coast, engaging in occasional heavy fighting at individual seaside villages. By evening it was in position to advance north toward the 36th Division.

The situation at the Camel beaches on the right was decidedly different. The Allies wanted to assault Camel Red beach at the head of the Gulf of Fréjus, for it provided good access into the interior. But it was too well defended to be attacked frontally. They therefore decided to have the 36th Division land at two smaller beaches farther east first and not attempt to take Camel Red until later in the day.

One of them, Camel Blue beach to the east, near Anthéor, was surrounded by permanent as well as field fortifications. This tiny, sand beach, barely 100 yards long and 30 yards wide, was located at the end of a cove with steep and rocky cliffs rising from three sides. Behind one of the cliffs was a high viaduct carrying the main rail line between Nice and Marseilles. At 8:00 A.M., one battalion of the 141st Regimental Combat Team struck the Anthéor beach in the face of strong artillery fire. The barrage was so heavy that the Americans had to call on naval gun support to help dislodge the enemy. By midday the battalion had captured the heights above the beach and began following the coast road north and east. The attached tanks and tank destroyers found the going difficult, for sections of the road at the base of the steep hills had been dynamited, and bulldozers had to be brought in to clear them. Reducing the pillboxes along the coast also proved to be time-consuming work, but by nightfall the battalion had still advanced about five miles.

The other small beach, Camel Green, was well defended with antitank, mortar, and artillery batteries as well as infantry concealed in seaside villas, concrete bunkers, and personnel trenches. The beach's most prominent feature was Cap Drammont, a red cliff which jutted into the sea on the right with a lighthouse perched on a small island offshore. Behind the narrow sand and shingle beach was piled quarried rock with a coastal road and railway just beyond.

The other two battalions of the 141st Regiment landed at Camel Green beach amidst concentrated enemy fire. Two landing craft were sunk before they ever reached shore, and another burst into flames just as it began to unload. But most of the troops were able to land unscathed. One battalion passed through the small village of Drammont on the right, cleared the cape, met the battalion which had landed on Camel Blue beach, and moved inland to assist in the drive east in the direction of Cannes.

The other battalion which came ashore on Drammont beach quickly set up a roadblock and occupied the heights overlooking the beach area. It then held its position while the 143rd Regiment, which had landed about ten o'clock, passed through on the left to move in the direction of Saint-Raphaël. The battalion of the 141st then headed east through Agay to join the other battalions in its regiment. The 143rd experienced hard fighting east and north of Saint-Raphaël and was not able to occupy the town until the next morning.

In the meantime, measures were being undertaken to reduce the German defenses on Camel Red beach, where the 142nd Regiment was scheduled to land at 2:00 P.M. At eleven, minesweepers moved forward through the Gulf of Fréjus, but were shelled and forced to retire. Shortly afterward, heavy bombers dropped 187 tons of explosives on the enemy's positions. The minesweepers returned and swept the beaches up to 500 yards from shore in spite of heavy fire. Naval guns then opened up, and two demolition teams in scout boats and twelve drone boats were sent in (only three of the latter exploded properly). Troops were loaded into assault craft and were waiting for instructions to move through the water toward the beach. But enemy fire still did not abate.

Rear Adm. Spencer S. Lewis, who was in charge of the Camel beach landings, saw from his flagship that the situation was critical.[18] In his view, the attacking force was headed for disaster. General Dahlquist, the 36th Division commander, was already ashore and in no position to make a decision. Admiral Lewis therefore ordered the landing craft group to change its plans (in some cases the message was relayed by megaphone to the assault boats) and to land on the much smaller Drammont beach on the right. This they did, and the 142nd started coming ashore at 3:15, more than an hour late, but without loss. Later that day Dahlquist signaled Admiral Lewis thanking him for taking the initiative. But General Truscott, the head of VI Corps, was not at all pleased.[19] He felt that by not landing on Camel Red beach, the 142nd had delayed clearing the beach for supplies and had prevented the quick capture of an airfield near Fréjus. In his opinion, the inevitable result of not taking Camel Red beach that afternoon would be to slow up the penetration inland. At one point he even called for Dahlquist's removal, but was persuaded by General Devers not to relieve him.[20]

Having landed at Drammont beach, the 142nd Regiment was now approximately ten miles east of Fréjus, its immediate objective. The troops moved off in column along a secondary road swinging north around Saint-Raphaël, and headed for Fréjus, which lay about a mile inland from the coast. General Dahlquist hoped his force could make up for lost time and capture the town that night, but this proved impossible, and it was not taken until the sixteenth.

One of the more amusing incidents of the first day took place on the road to Fréjus.[21] About dusk a company of Americans came upon a resort area. After they had passed some of the buildings they came to a house. Several of the troops decided to go in and investigate it more thoroughly. The intelligence officer later reported: "As they entered the gate a woman came from the house and stated that she had fifteen German soldiers disarmed and locked in her garage. . . . The prisoners were taken from the garage and turned over to me for interrogation. . . . The prisoners stated that they were going inland to join their organization in Frejus. They had stopped in the house, possibly to hide, and in some way or other she had disarmed them and locked them up."

Similar incidents occurred at other places on invasion day, but in general the landings took place against relatively light opposition with only occasional flurries of heavy fighting. The German reaction was weak, not because they were unaware of what was happening, but because they were in no position to defend the coast properly. The defensive forces grouped around Toulon and Marseilles for the most part had no alternative but to stay where they were. Reinforcements from west of the Rhône—the 11th Panzer and the 198th Infantry—were only beginning to move across the river.[22] All possible reserves east of the Rhône—two infantry battalions, two antitank companies, an antiaircraft unit, and two more infantry battalions from Marseilles—were gathered together at Aix-en-Provence during the morning of the fifteenth. Commanded by Brigadier General von Schwerin, the battle group headed east along Highway 7 toward Le Muy to counter the airborne assault, but they did not meet the Allies until the next day.

The air and naval reaction was equally feeble. The local Luftwaffe commander was unwilling to risk using his attack planes until the evening of the fifteenth. About dusk one of seven Dornier 217s scored a direct hit on an LST 600 yards off Saint-Raphaël, inflicting fifty-five casualties. Altogether on the fifteenth German air activity was confined to twenty-one sorties, mostly reconnaissance flights. The German navy sent out some ships and patrol boats, but they confined their activities to the "fringes" and did not attack the main invasion convoys.

In comparison, Allied air and naval forces were unbelievably active.[23] As soon as the first waves were ashore, bombers and fighter bombers instituted their post-H-hour plan, Operation Ducrot, and launched air strikes against strongpoints and road bridges from Nice to Toulon. They kept up their activity throughout the day. The same applied to the P–38s,

P–47s, and Spitfires, which attacked enemy gun positions in the assault area and patrolled the beaches, the Spitfires above 22,000 feet, the American fighters below. British Beaufighters assumed the patrol duties at night. At the same time, British Seafires and US Hellcats and Wildcats flew 287 sorties off the decks of the nine carriers, located thirty miles from shore. The navy support force was also exceedingly busy, firing round after round against enemy positions and maintaining a screen of PT boats and up to twenty destroyers to protect the invasion fleet. The Germans were obviously outmatched at sea and in the air.

The results at the end of the first day were indeed gratifying. Allied aircraft had flown 3,936 Dragoon-related sorties. This number, combined with 313 non-Dragoon sorties, made it the greatest one-day air effort in the Mediterranean theater to date. The navy had also fulfilled its numerous tasks admirably. It had landed approximately 12,800 personnel on Alpha beaches, 33,000 on Delta, and 14,350 on Camel, for a total of 60,150. Vehicles numbering 6,737 had also been brought ashore. This had been accomplished without the use of Camel Red beach, which was scheduled to be one of the main supply beaches. (It was not cleared of mines and ready for cargo until the eighteenth.) Naval ship losses were surprisingly small—one LST and four landing craft destroyed, two ships and twenty-four landing craft damaged.

It was also a highly successful day for the army. The airborne and seaborne landings, the most vulnerable portion of the operation, had taken place without serious mishap and with only light casualties. To be sure, the assault on Camel Red beach had had to be abandoned, and the troops slated to land there shifted elsewhere. But, nonetheless, large numbers of combat personnel had gotten ashore and had pushed inland and along the coast at a rapid rate. By nightfall some of the units had advanced as far as ten miles from the invasion beaches. German resistance had generally been light, though the enemy had engaged the Allies in fierce fighting at such places as Cap Cavalaire, east of Saint-Raphaël, and near Théoule-sur-Mer. It had also taken the Allies some time to dig the enemy out of numerous buildings and strongpoints. At day's end, they had taken 2,041 prisoners, including numerous Armenian and Russian troops. American losses were 198 killed, captured, or missing, and 399 wounded. (French casualties, though proportionally higher, are not recorded.)

General Dahlquist summed up the views of many of the commanders when he wrote to his wife several days after the invasion: "So far it has been a fine victory. We did our job, . . . with relatively few casualties and we have captured a tremendous number of prisoners."[24] An August 16 editorial in the *New York Times* was more effusive in its appraisal:

> Striking another mortal blow at Nazi Germany, a new Allied army has stormed ashore on the beaches of southern France to establish the fourth major front in Europe. Brilliantly conceived, brilliantly executed and brilliantly timed, the new invasion is another stirring demonstration of the grand Allied strategy of constant attack, which is the secret of victory. It is also a demonstration of the still rising tide of Allied power, which can select its own time and place to strike. It is above all a demonstration of the desperate straits to which Hitler has been reduced.[25]

On the sixteenth, D + 1, the Allied advance continued, but in the face of stiffening opposition.[26] In one of the first encounters of the day, four tanks, four tank destroyers, and a company of infantry troops reduced a German roadblock at daybreak to allow portions of the 3rd Division to move west along the coast. Farther inland, the 3rd's 30th Regiment occupied Pierrefeu, a village eleven miles northwest of the invasion beaches.

The 45th Division in the center recorded the most spectacular gains of the day. One battalion of the 157th Regiment pushed toward Vidauban, along Highway 7, another battalion ran into the German battle group which had been assembled the day before at Aix-en-Provence, and the Americans were forced to halt until the seventeenth, by which time the enemy had started to pull back. Despite the hold up, the Americans by now had effectively penetrated the Maures mountains and were twenty miles inland.

Other "Thunderbird" formations cleared Saint-Aygulf, after bitter fighting, along the coast. The theater history records a portion of what happened. "Casualties for the 1st Bn [180th Regiment] were heavy as individual strongpoints were attacked and overcome. The morning of 16 Aug Co B forced its way into St. Aygulf. As Sgt Mario R Marias led his platoon forward through mined approaches, he fired his submachine gun at enemy snipers and threw grenades into doorways. Sgt Marias killed three of the enemy and forced the surrender of six."[27] The advance continued throughout the day. By evening, the 45th was in contact with the 36th Division in the Argens River valley and the 1st Airborne Task Force southwest of Le Muy.

The British and American paratroopers also had an eventful day, capturing Le Muy and Draguignan and taking more than 300 prisoners in each instance. The main prize at Draguignan, a French governmental center north of Le Muy, was the overrunning of the German LXII Corps headquarters and its elimination as a command post. (The corps commander, Maj. Gen. Ferdinand Neuling, and some others managed to escape, but they were apprehended farther north on the eighteenth.) Portions of the 36th Division to the east took Saint-Raphaël and Fréjus in the morning, reassembled, and moved north and west toward Le Muy to establish contact with the airborne force. This was accomplished on the seventeenth. The 141st Regiment pushed east along Highway 98 and contacted the survivors of the French marine assault group, which had run into severe difficulties early on invasion day. The regiment then passed through Théoule-sur-Mer about midnight on the road to Cannes.

The navy and air force kept up their offensive pressure, too.[28] Naval gunfire raked the coast, especially on the flanks. Allied aircraft, including 128 carrier planes, concentrated their efforts on targets in the Rhône delta and for some miles up the river. Fifty-one British Wellingtons and seven Halifaxes from Italy attacked an airfield near Valence, and 108 B–17 Fortresses dropped 293 tons of bombs on four main bridges. In both cases the results were disappointing because of poor visibility. One-hundred-twenty-nine medium bombers also struck other targets in the Rhône delta. In addition, on the sixteenth, XII Tactical Air Command flew 1,250 sorties against enemy targets, and American, British, and French fighter pilots undertook about 700 sorties of a patrol, escort, and reconnaissance nature.

While American troops fanned out to the west, north, and east, French forces began to come ashore at Cavalaire Bay and across the Delta beaches east of Sainte-Maxime.[29] At noon, the 1st Combat Command, part of the 1st Armored Division, was the first to disembark. Originally this 4,000-man force was to assist the 36th Division on the right, but because of the problem at Camel Red beach, it was now placed under General Eagles's 45th Division. Following at 8:00 P.M. were the 1st Motorized Infantry and the 3rd Algerian divisions. Although each of them possessed a full complement of approximately 16,500 troops and 3,053 vehicles, only a portion of their soldiers and equipment were unloaded on the sixteenth. There was only one mishap during the disembarkation: the Algerian formation was attacked by German bombers and suffered eighty casualties.

The next day another 4,000 soldiers of the 1st Armored Division and additional 1st Infantry and 3rd Algerian troops came ashore, and on the eighteenth, portions of the 9th Colonial Division, two groups of Tabors (with more than 1,500 mules), and a special shock battalion arrived two days earlier than planned. With this force, comprising most of the II French Corps, General de Lattre (who had the American diplomat William Bullitt on his staff) hoped to liberate at all speed the ports of Toulon and Marseilles to the west. The other three divisions which made up French Army B were not to arrive until later.

Another French contribution was also becoming evident by this time. The French Resistance in the Midi, like their counterparts farther north during the Normandy campaign, had prepared their forces for a significant role in Dragoon. The radio message, "Nancy has a stiff neck—the huntsman is hungry—Gaby is going to lie down in the grass," was the signal that the invasion would take place on the fifteenth, and Resistance units went into action.[30] They helped the attackers in a myriad of ways—pointing out enemy minefields and other entrapments, infiltrating behind the lines to provide up-to-date combat intelligence, remaining behind to help run the liberated towns and villages. They assisted further inland as well by such acts as disrupting rail and road traffic, cutting telephone and telegraph lines, and attacking troop concentrations. An early example of the type of activities in which the Resistance engaged occurred on the sixteenth at Larche on the Italian border. In this instance, a garrison of Polish troops was forced to surrender after being subverted by a woman agent. Numerous other acts of bravery and cunning were to follow in the days ahead.

Also by the sixteenth an atmosphere of triumph and jubilation was beginning to pervade the liberated areas along the Provençal coast. At 9:00 A.M., General Patch, wearing his usual violet scarf and combat helmet, and accompanied by Admiral Hewitt, French Adm. André Lemonnier, and United States Secretary of the Navy James Forrestal, went ashore on one of the Delta beaches.[31] Symbolically, Lemonnier touched French soil first. They visited General Truscott at his VI Corps headquarters near Sainte-Maxime, returned to the USS *Catoctin* just after noon, and conferred with two of the overall Mediterranean commanders, Field Marshal Wilson and Adm. Sir John Cunningham while aboard ship. During the afternoon, Patch returned to shore, this time to the Camel beach area. From there he and General Dahlquist rode through the recently captured towns of Saint-Raphaël and Fréjus amid shouts of "Vive les Américains" and the singing of the long-forbidden "Marseillaise." That same afternoon, Seventh Army established its headquarters in a hotel west of Saint-Tropez. The Allied forces were there to stay.

By the seventeenth, the immediate Allied objective of penetrating the coastal hills and reaching the Blue Line, twenty miles from the invasion beaches, had been attained, and American troops began pushing steadily north and west. Their goal at this point was not so much to cut off the enemy as it was to maneuver their forces into positions from where the Germans *could* be cut off. To accomplish this task, the 3rd Division was to shift its center of attack north toward Highway 7 and move west toward Brignoles. French forces were to fill in the area near the coast vacated by the 3rd Division and from there take the offensive against Toulon. In the center, the 45th Division was to form the point of the wedge and advance from Le Luc northwest toward Barjols. The "Texas" Division on the right was to secure the flank, and after being relieved by the 1st Airborne Task Force, move north toward Castellane, sixty miles inland. The main road in the area, Highway 85, was also known as the Route Napoléon, since it had been used by him after his escape from Elba to make his way to Paris in 1815.

The fighting during the next three days was at times scattered, at times heavy. But at no time were the Germans in a position to halt the Allied juggernaut more than temporarily. On the left, portions of the 3rd Division, at Saint-Honoré and La Londe near the coast, met strong resistance, which was not overcome until the night of the seventeenth. Most of the American forces then headed north toward Highway 7. They were greeted by two battalions of the 30th Regiment, which, along with elements of the 45th Division, had taken Le Luc the previous day and advanced west toward Brignoles. At Brignoles the Germans, including portions of Battle Group von Schwerin, put up stout resistance. Several battalions of the 3rd Division began attacking the German positions at 7:00 A.M. on the eighteenth, but the enemy held out throughout the day. By evening, however, the Americans had surrounded the town and then captured it the next morning. Soon afterwards, other units, including the 1st French Combat Command, began streaming west along Highway 7 in the direction of the major road and rail center at Aix-en-Provence.

The goal of the 45th Division, after helping to clear Le Luc, was to reach and cross the Durance River, which runs west out of the Provence Alps and empties into the Rhône at Avignon. On the way, portions of the 179th regiment ran into a roadblock immediately east of the town of Barjols. Barjols is located in mountainous terrain, just north of the headwaters of the Argens River and fifty miles by road west of Saint-Raphaël. French partisans in the town were reportedly fighting an estimated 300 Wehrmacht troops, and the Americans were asked to help out. On the eighteenth, after a preliminary artillery barrage, three American companies attacked German hill positions east and north of Barjols throughout the day, but they were unable to dislodge the enemy. The theater history describes the action that followed:

All companies dug in for the night; after dark wire was run and supplies brought up. Enemy vehicular movement on roads leading out of Barjols was heard during the night.

The morning of 19 August the attack was renewed. All companies in position—A, C, and I—fought to occupy high ground and reverse slopes in front of them. Co B with a platoon of tanks made a wide sweep to the north behind Co C to come in on Barjols from the rear. The tanks had trouble with the terrain and received some mortar fire, but the advance continued. By 1030 Co B had started the swing, and the Germans were pulling out of town by the road to the southwest. Artillery observation on the hills east of Barjols brought down heavy fire on the retreating enemy. The road block was cleared by tanks at 1120 as infantrymen swarmed into town. Barjols had fallen.[32]

Meanwhile, other elements of the "Thunderbird" Division bypassed Barjols, pushed west through Rians, and by the twentieth were astride the Durance River, fourteen miles northeast of Aix-en-Provence. The invasion was becoming a rout.

In the 36th Division area on the right, two important developments took place. One was the formation of an armored task force under Brig. Gen. Frederick B. Butler, Truscott's chief of staff. Plans had already been made before the invasion to establish such a force, if necessary, to take advantage of any gap in enemy lines. This took on special urgency when it was decided to switch the 1st French Combat Command, which possessed a long strike capability, from the United States VI Corps to de Lattre's French Army B. Butler's task force started assembling near Le Muy on the seventeenth. It was made up of a tank battalion, an infantry battalion (from the 36th), a field artillery battalion, a tank destroyer company, a cavalry reconnaissance squadron, and engineering and medical companies. Its mission was to reconnoiter north in force, contact the French Resistance in the area, and then await further orders. Its eventual objective, though not stated at the time, was to cut off the enemy, if possible, before he could undertake a successful retreat. At 5:30 A.M. on the eighteenth, Task Force Butler began moving west and north and reached Riez by nightfall. The next day, it continued its northerly advance toward Sisteron along Napoleonic Highway 85.

In the other major development, the 1st Airborne Task Force relieved two 36th Division regiments on the eastern flank, and the entire division then prepared to follow Task Force Butler north. Its only combat of any consequence was on the nineteenth, when a specially formed unit came to the relief of an isolated pocket of paratroopers east of Fayence.

In the meantime, the II French Corps was being readied for action.[33] Rather than forming near the beaches, General de Lattre decided to have them assemble in a forward area near Collobrières. At one point General Truscott suggested to Patch that the United States 3rd Division might undertake the attack against Toulon rather than French forces as originally envisaged. But the Seventh Army commander decided to have the French go ahead (de Lattre had already formulated the tactical plan), and on the nineteenth, reinforced by the 1st Combat Command under General Sudre, the II Corps was ready to assume the offensive.

Between the seventeenth and the nineteenth, Allied ships and aircraft also continued their offensive missions.[34] During the night of the sixteenth, the navy carried out a successful diversionary attack at La Ciotat between Toulon and Marseilles. The operation netted 210 prisoners and sank two enemy corvettes. More generally, the navy continued to help protect the invasion beaches, but by the eighteenth most of the naval gunfire support had been shifted to the flanks. The large ships undertook to reduce the town of Hyères and the island of Porquerolles, east of Toulon. (Hyères fell to French troops on August 21, but the German garrison on Porquerolles held out until the twenty-second.) At the same time, the bombardment of Toulon itself began in earnest with both naval and air force units taking part. On the nineteenth they sank (both claimed credit) the demobilized battleship *Strasbourg* and a cruiser and a U-boat, in the harbor area.

In addition to attacking Toulon (and Marseilles), the air force devoted its effort mainly to bombing various transportation targets, enemy airfields, and the Rhône bridges. After the sixteenth, the strategic bombers returned to their primary mission of hitting factories in Germany and the Ploesti oil fields, but the B–25s remained to attack nine Rhône bridges over a four-day period. The results were disappointing for reconnaissance photos indicated that while all of them were damaged, only two had been rendered unserviceable. Fighters and fighter bombers (including carrier planes) concentrated on gun positions, radar sites, and road and rail columns, "finding many favorable targets in the rapidly retreating enemy ground troops because of a complete lack of enemy fighter opposition." Although XII Tactical Air Command fighters from Corsica did attack German airfields on several occasions, Allied actions did not prevent five JU–88s from bombing the flagship *Catoctin* at dusk on the eighteenth and causing six deaths and wounding forty-two. Nevertheless, in spite of this incident, for all practical purposes Allied air and naval superiority was now unchallenged.

Having failed to stop the Allies, the Germans now made the only logical decision still open to them: They began a full-scale retreat. On the night of the seventeenth, Army

Task Force G received an order from Armed Forces High Command, which stipulated that all Wehrmacht forces and others associated with the German war effort were to evacuate all of southern France, from the Atlantic coast to the Italian border.[35] The only exceptions were the major ports—Toulon and Marseilles in the Mediterranean, and La Rochelle and Royan at the mouth of the Gironde River along the Bay of Biscay coast. Their retention was to deny them to the Allies, and typically, they were to be held to the last man. The order did not go into detail, but it directed that the withdrawal take place in stages with the eventual goal of linking with Army Group B near Dijon in eastern France.

General Blaskowitz and General Wiese, the Nineteenth Army commander, immediately began to implement the order. Except for the 148th and the 157th Reserve divisions, which were to be placed under the German commander in Italy, the Wehrmacht formations were to retreat up the Rhône. Most of the 11th Panzer, 198th Infantry, and 338th Infantry divisions were finally east of the river, and they were formed into a screening force to cover the withdrawal.[36] On the nineteenth, the 198th occupied forward positions east of Aix-en-Provence, but two days later it was forced back, and elements of all three divisions established a defensive line southeast of Avignon. The 244th and 242nd divisions as well as numerous naval personnel remained at Marseilles and Toulon to face the inevitable siege of their cities. Between August 16 and 18, the Luftwaffe managed to marshal its remaining fourteen Do–217s, sixty-five Ju–88s, and fighters in the area and launched approximately 140 sorties against Allied targets. But by the twenty-first the Luftwaffe had begun to evacuate their bases, and German air activity in Provence, except for an occasional reconnaissance flight, had ceased to exist.[37] Also by this date the few enemy naval vessels that were left had been formed into a Rhône flotilla for ferrying duty, were bottled up in Toulon harbor, or stationed in Italian ports.

Did the Allies know of German intentions for a full-scale withdrawal? The answer is yes.[38] A Seventh Army message issued to the troops on the twentieth, two-and-a-half days after the German order, acknowledged that the enemy, except along the coast, was in retreat. This may have been the result of good combat intelligence. Or it may have been a reflection of the offensive spirit which pervaded the Dragoon operation, what General Eaker termed an impressive display of "aggressiveness and willingness to fight." But it is most likely that General Patch knew of the German order to withdraw through Ultra. The British had decoded the German message early on the afternoon of the eighteenth. At about this same time First Sea Lord Sir Andrew Cunningham wrote in his diary, "There is a rumour that the Germans have orders to pull back while holding Marseilles and Toulon." With access to Ultra secrets, Cunningham must have known that the "rumor" had a good deal of substance behind it. This information was dispatched from London to the theater with all speed, and it leaves little doubt that the Mediterranean commanders knew what the Wehrmacht was up to. Now, they felt, was the time to exploit their advantage to the fullest.

During the early post-invasion phase, the Allies also set about reorganizing their air and ground components and developing their lines of supply.[39] The army reorganization involved mainly the shifting of units, such as the 1st Airborne relieving the 36th Division and the II French Corps taking its position on the left of the American forces. But other events should be noted as well. The 2nd British Parachute Brigade returned to Alexander's forces in Italy, and additional French formations began to arrive. And since Dragoon was not in jeopardy, Allied plans to rush, if necessary, three divisions—the 44th, 100th, and 103rd—from the United States were set aside, and provisions made to ship the troops to southern France on a less hurried basis.

The air reorganization was more extensive. The Americans were advancing at such a rapid rate that they would soon be beyond the range of Corsica-based fighters. Hence the need was great to take over quickly existing airfields or to build new ones. On the nineteenth, just four days after the invasion, the first squadron of Spitfires started to operate from airfields on the mainland, and three more airstrips were to be ready within the coming week. Nevertheless, the constantly changing bomb line coupled with poor coordination between XII Tactical Air Command and Seventh Army tended to hamper the close air support effort in a number of instances.

The assault beaches obviously changed in appearance, too. Since the Allies did not expect to take Toulon or Marseilles for some weeks, supplies initially were to be landed across the beaches. While the Americans provided most of the service troops, British, French, and Italian units also did their part. In spite of their prodigious efforts, problems were bound to ensue.[40] A British lieutenant commander, for example, sent a scathing report to his superiors decrying the lack of facilities for his personnel, who had to sleep in the rain with no tents, while the Americans enjoyed every amenity imaginable—a large "mother" ship, beach tents, well-cooked and hot food, clean and suitable clothing. There was also the problem of adapting supplies to the combat situation. Supply officers had expected extended fighting near the beaches, and they therefore assured that large amounts of ammunition and large numbers of tanks and tank destroyers were available. But with the rapid push inland, the main need was for trucks and gasoline, not ammunition and half-tracks. Finally, troops in the rear areas, in search of "fun," could not always be restrained from looting private homes and commandeering vehicles which belonged to French citizens. But all in all, the Allies had every reason to view the first four days of Dragoon as an outstanding success. American divisions had advanced into the interior, in some cases as far as sixty miles, and had made extensive gains along the coast. French forces were already moving into position to attack Toulon, and the French "bonus," the Resistance, was proving its worth. Allied ships and aircraft had swept away their meager opposition and had attained mastery of the sea and air.

Specifically, by the twentieth, 114,850 personnel, 17,247 vehicles, and 44,851 tons of stores had been unloaded over the beaches.[41] Allied casualties totaled only 1,966, including 1,395 American (through the seventeenth), while the number of enemy captured had risen to approximately 14,000 prisoners.

General Eisenhower, who in his own way had helped launch Dragoon, showed his elation with the early results by sending a telegram to Field Marshal Wilson for Prime Minister Churchill, then in Italy, whose distaste for the operation had not prevented him from "stopping by" to witness the event. "Will you please pass the following to the Prime Minister. I am delighted to note in your latest telegram to me that you have personally and legally adopted the Dragoon. I am sure he will grow fat and prosperous under your watchfulness. If you can guarantee that your presence at all such operations will have the same effect that it did in this wonderful show, I will make sure that in any future operations in this theater you are given a fleet of your own.—Ike"[42] In subsequent months, Churchill returned to his earlier skepticism regarding Dragoon, but at the time he undoubtedly did enjoy watching quite a "good show."

5

The Chase

O N AUGUST 19, four days after the invasion, Patch's Seventh Army headquarters issued Field Order No. 2.[1] Though soon overtaken by events, and more cautious in tone than subsequent orders, it is important because it set the immediate objectives which the Allies hoped to accomplish: French Army B was to push west and capture Toulon and Marseilles without delay, while part of Truscott's VI Corps was to move west and seize Aix-en-Provence, with other elements advancing north to secure crossings over the Durance River and then continue advancing along Highway 85 to Sisteron. Though he did not specify what was to happen next, Truscott had in mind that some of the American forces would then move quickly either north toward Grenoble or west to the Rhône River, to cut off the main portion of the German forces fleeing north. In the east, the 1st Airborne Task Force was to secure a defensive line west of Cannes.

In a larger sense, Patch's August 19 order was significant because it signaled the end of the assault phase of Dragoon and the beginning of the clearing of the main Mediterranean ports and the push north. Whether the American and

French advance would be rapid enough to deal a defeated, dispirited, and thought-to-be disorganized foe a crushing blow depended on two conflicting factors: the ability of the Allies to sustain their early momentum, versus the skill of the Wehrmacht to resist and evade capture. These antagonisms dominated the fighting in the days and weeks ahead.

The objective of de Lattre's French Army B—to liberate Toulon and Marseilles—was not expected to be an easy task.[2] Allied planners had long thought that a land attack against the ports was the most practical approach, since both were heavily defended from the seaward side. Two east-west highways provided the best access to them through the Aleppo pine and chestnut-covered hills. One was coastal Highway 98, which continued west from La Londe through Hyères to Toulon. The second, farther inland, passed through Collobrières to Solliès-Pont, then northwest to Meounes and straight west through Aubagne to Marseilles. In between were various north-south roads which could be used to move troops and supplies, if necessary, from one of the lateral routes to the other. The distance from Toulon to Marseilles by road was approximately forty miles. Fortified heights north of Toulon and north and east of Marseilles were the main defenses to be overcome, although the eastern suburbs of Marseilles were also well fortified.

De Lattre's tactical plan was to have French forces move rapidly to encircle, isolate, and penetrate these two renowned cities from three sides, thereby bringing about their quick capitulation. For the attack against Toulon, the 1st French, 9th Colonial, and part of the 3rd Algerian divisions were to be the main units involved. They were to be assisted by a number of special forces—a Senegalese rifle battalion, a shock battalion, a Moroccan Tabor *goum* (similar in size to a company), and the commando group which had secured the Allies' western flank on invasion day. (De Lattre also wanted

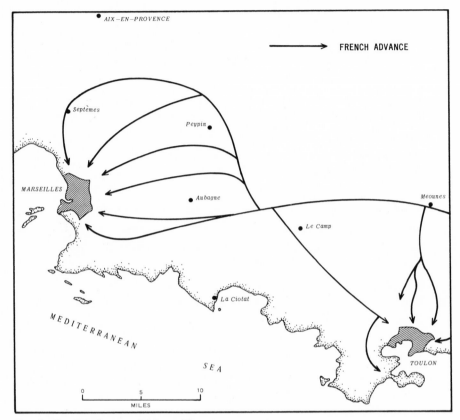

Battle for Toulon and Marseilles

to utilize French paratroopers, but De Gaulle ordered them to be kept in reserve.)

De Lattre did not intend to wait until Toulon was taken before attacking Marseilles. He assigned the Marseilles operation to the main portion of the 3rd Algerian Division, two groups of Tabors, and two combat commands of the 1st Armored Division. In addition, he was given General Sudre's 1st Combat Command, which had been shifted from the United States VI Corps to de Lattre's control on the nineteenth. At the time it was reassigned, it had been serving as a screening force along Highway 7 to the north of General O'Daniel's 3rd Division. The French commander could also count on considerable help from the Resistance forces and from the massive Allied naval and air contingents.

In general, the German forces on the outskirts and inside the two cities were expected to give a good account of themselves. Elements of the 244th Division at Marseilles and the 242nd Division at Toulon were among the better formations in the area, well-trained and well-disciplined. The naval and army personnel who manned the artillery guns and performed other duties plus diverse other forces brought the total to approximately 18,000 troops in each area.³ Besides the not inconsiderable former French defenses, the Germans had added some of their own after they had occupied the Vichy zone in November 1942. In March 1944 Hitler had declared Marseilles and Toulon to be defense areas, which meant they were to be prepared for all-around defense. Though still incomplete by August, numerous field and permanent fortifications had been constructed. The troops themselves had anticipated being cut off and had been directed to stockpile large amounts of ammunition and material and to secure their water supplies so as to withstand a long siege.

On the nineteenth General Brosset's 1st French Division

moved out along the coast road in the direction of Toulon. As the troops approached the town of Hyères, they were met by German artillery and antitank fire, which was especially heavy from the heights north of town. This hill mass was important, for it lay above the coast road and dominated the approaches from both the east and the west. A regiment of the 1st French Division was detached north and started encircling the strongly fortified positions. By the next day, Hyères had been cut off from the north and east. The isolation of the town was completed when the 9th Colonial Division, moving southwest along Highway 97 toward Toulon, blocked any possible enemy retreat to the northwest.

In the meantime, the main body of the 1st Division was making a frontal assault against Hyères from the east. One group encountered exceptionally heavy fire, including two antitank and three antiaircraft guns, near the Golf Hotel, just northeast of the city. The French commander withdrew the infantry elements from the immediate area, and called in three battalions of artillery to neutralize the strongpoint. At point-blank range of less than 1,000 yards, the French 105s and 155s fired approximately 1,000 rounds but registered only 100 direct hits.

The Germans tenaciously held on, even though the Allies were now directing additional supporting fire from their large naval ships against the town. On the twenty-first, a French battalion, after fierce, hand-to-hand fighting, was able to close to within fifty yards of the hotel. And early in the evening, a bayonet charge finally overran the strongpoint. Besides finding many Germans dead, the French took 140 prisoners. That same evening the 1st Division passed through Hyères on the road to Toulon. One motorized battalion remained behind to help Resistance forces with mopping up operations. (Nearby to the south, on the twenty-second, naval gunfire induced what was left of a German garrison on the island of Porquerolles to surrender, and the next day, 190 Senegalese soldiers landed on the Giens Peninsula, and with the help of the Resistance, cleared that neck of land south of Hyères.)

Toulon, one of de Lattre's two prime objectives, lies in a bay surrounded to the north and east by wooded hills. To the south, it is protected by the thumblike Saint-Mandrier Peninsula, which sticks out into the sea in front of the harbor. The Germans, like the French before them, had used Toulon's natural defenses to good advantage. The heights above the city are dominated by three hills, Monts Caumes, Faron, and Coudon. All three had been made into heavily fortified strongpoints. The Saint-Mandrier Peninsula, which covered the sea approaches to this famous naval base, was a veritable armed camp. Within a two-mile-square area, the Germans had placed eighteen batteries with fifty-four guns, ranging in caliber from 75 to 340 mm ("Big Willie") and seventeen antiaircraft pieces.[4] The batteries had been connected by a maze of tunnels which were then linked to living quarters, electric power plants, and ammunition depots below ground. An underground area for midget submarines, a seaplane base, and a fueling station were also located on the peninsula.

The defenses inside Toulon itself were also formidable. All approaches to the city were blocked by antitank obstacles, pillboxes, and minefields. The numerous artillery batteries (totaling approximately 150 guns), blockhouses, and firing trenches were protected by mines, barbed wire, and other entanglements. The Germans had also taken special care to see that four forts within the city were well defended.

The envelopment of Toulon began on August 20, one day before the fall of Hyères. Five battle groups were assigned the task. Brosset's 1st Division, after taking Hyères, was to advance on Toulon from the east. To its right, the 9th

Colonial Division, which had captured Solliès-Pont on the twentieth, was to proceed southwest toward Toulon along Highway 97. The third group, part of the 3rd Algerian Division, named the Linarès and Bonjour groups after their commanders, and a *goum* of Tabors, had moved north and were to approach Toulon from the heights above the city. The fourth group, the rest of the 3rd Algerian, the 1st Armored Division, and two *goums* of Tabors, formed a screening force to the north. They were also to push west in the direction of Marseilles. The final group, including the Senegalese, shock battalions, and the commando group, was to be used for special missions, thus giving the French field commanders additional flexibility.

As General Magnan's 9th Colonial Division approached Mont Coudon, northeast of the city, it came under heavy artillery fire. The commando group was given the job of dislodging the enemy from the heights, which General de Lattre has described as "a fortified rock, 2,300 ft. high, rising from the plain like the prow of a gigantic ship."[5] On the morning of the twenty-first, the commandos began assaulting the enemy positions. It was slow going, but by midafternoon, with the aid of rocket fire and grenades, most of the ridgeline had been taken. Only a fort on the eastern end of the strongpoint held out. At 5:00 P.M., the German sailors who were manning the fort indicated their desire to capitulate. But while some of the commandos were scaling the walls by rope to receive the surrender, the Germans inside signaled an artillery battery nearby to open fire on the fort. The result was the death of a number of Germans and French alike. The theater history relates the next and final act. "After enemy firing had ceased, the commandos put a heavy mortar in position and were also to knock out two German 100 mm guns camouflaged in an orchard below."[6] For all practical purposes, Mont Coudon was now in French hands, although several enemy attempts to recapture the heights had to be beaten back during the next three days.

To the northwest, the 3rd Algerian Division's Linarès Group, reinforced by the shock battalion, infiltrated south through the mountains and on the twenty-second captured the German strongpoints of Monts Caumes and Faron. Despite violent counterattacks, the French continued to hold on to the heights which overlooked the city. Toulon had been effectively cut off from the north.

The rest of the 3rd Algerian Division had continued west along a northern road toward Marseilles. On the twentieth, when they reached the crossroads town of Le Camp, the Bonjour Group was detached, and after clearing a roadblock, it pushed southeast along Highway 8, the main road linking Toulon with Marseilles. By the twenty-second they had reached the outskirts of Toulon itself. That same day, the blocking of a coastal road by a tank destroyer battalion completed the isolation of the city from the west.

To the east, the 9th Colonial and 1st French divisions, led by General Larminat, continued to advance, but in the face of stiff opposition. The final barrier in front of the city was the suburb of La Valette, and it took the French two days, with tanks and Senegalese troops spearheading the attack, to capture the town. But by the twenty-third, they were ready to assault the city proper.

In effect, the French had Toulon surrounded. The 9th Colonial and First divisions were located to the east; the Linarès group, shock troops, and Tabors to the north; the Bonjour Group to the west. The 242nd German Division and its associated units braced themselves to meet the onslaught from their prepared, inner defenses.

On the morning of the twenty-third, with the assistance of artillery and naval gunfire, the 9th Colonial and 1st divisions began penetrating the eastern sections of the city. By

5:00 P.M., advance elements had reached the center of Toulon. At this point an unexpected event occurred. "Major Victor Mirkin moved up with two tanks to the Military Arsenal in the Le Mourillon sector of the city. He entered the arsenal and told the German commander that unless he surrendered immediately the fire of Allied warships would be brought down on the garrison. The commander capitulated, surrendering 17 officers and 800 men."[7]

On the twenty-fourth, similar incidents took place throughout the city. By evening, the Germans at three of the four main inner forts had surrendered. Still, pockets of resistance, especially near the docks, held out, and it was not until the twenty-sixth that the last enemy strongpoint in the city had been overrun. The French citizenry, in their elation, could not wait and held a victory parade the next day.

Their parade was premature because approximately 1,800 German troops, though cut off, were still resisting on the Saint-Mandrier Peninsula across the harbor. Allied ships and aircraft had been subjecting the area to a murderous combination of bombs and shells for days, but the well-entrenched enemy, commanded by Admiral Ruhfus, had refused to give up. Particularly savage artillery duels had taken place between the "Big Willie" battery and the French battleship *Lorraine*, the USS *Nevada*, and HMS *Ramillies*, and the cruisers offshore. ("Big Willie," as it was called by American sailors, actually consisted of four 340 mm guns, removed from the French battleship *Provence*, but two of them had been sabotaged by French workers.) Finally late on the evening of the twenty-seventh Admiral Ruhfus agreed to surrender, effective at six o'clock the next morning. Toulon and its environs were once again under French sovereignty.

An epilogue, described by General de Lattre, occurred that same morning.[8] Since the peninsula was infested with minefields, the French desired a detailed plan showing their locations. At 8:00 A.M. on the twenty-eighth, de Lattre had Admiral Ruhfus brought to him and told him to produce the map within three hours. If, after that time, a single French soldier stepped on a German mine, he, Ruhfus, would be shot. Within three hours, the plan was in de Lattre's hands.

French planners originally intended for the screening force above Toulon to move west in the direction of Marseilles, but only for reconnaissance and covering purposes. Late on the nineteenth, however, General de Lattre, after consulting with General de Monsabert, the commander of the 3rd Algerian Division, decided that an opportunity presented itself and should not be missed. Therefore, simultaneous with the assault on Toulon, Marseilles was also to be attacked. The Chapius Group of the 3rd Algerian Division, the 1st Armored Division, and two groups of Tabors were entrusted with the initial thrust against the city. The tactics to be used were to be the same as those being employed at Hyères and Toulon—rapid encirclement, isolation, and penetration from all sides.

The old and famous port of Marseilles did not possess the natural defenses of Toulon, but there were hills to the southeast and the Etoile mountain chain to the north and east. The approaches to the harbor area, located in the western portion of the city, were well protected by two islands with strong forts on them and minefields, antisubmarine nets, and other defenses near the entrances. Shore defenses consisted of approximately 150 coastal artillery, antiaircraft, and railway guns, though some of these guns could be directed only against sea targets. Since Marseilles did not have an extensive system of hilltop fortresses, the Germans had emphasized erecting defensive barriers in the suburbs. On all the main roads leading into the city, a series of roadblocks and antitank mines had been emplaced. On that section of Highway 8 leading north to Aix-en-Provence concrete slabs and dragon teeth blocked the roadway flanked on both sides by an antitank wall six feet thick at its base. The towns of Peypin, to the northeast, and Aubagne, directly east of the city, were both strongly held with roadblocks with entrenched enemy troops behind them. Inside Marseilles, the heights surrounding Notre Dame de la Garde cathedral and the dock area were particularly well-defended.

General Monsabert, whose jolly appearance and white moustache belied a bold and aggressive fighter, led the French attacking force. He directed that the Chapius Group and most of General Sudre's 1st Combat Command advance along the Le Camp-Aubagne axis and assault Marseilles from the east. The Tabor groups were to head across country and cut off the city from the north and south. To protect the northern flank, Monsabert ordered General du Vigier's 2nd Combat Command to push north in the direction of the Rhône valley.

On the twenty-first, the Chapius Group and the 1st Combat Command ran into strong German roadblocks at Aubagne. The next day, while Sudre's armor tied down the enemy in front of the town, infantry elements swung north between the Aubagne and Peypin strongpoints and filtered through the Etoile mountain passes toward Marseilles. Some of the forces took a secondary road; others experienced a nine-hour climb over difficult terrain. But in neither instance did they encounter the enemy. By the evening of the twenty-second, advance elements of the 3rd Algerian Division were poised on the outskirts of the city.

In the meantime, garbed in their brown turbans and wool robes, the Tabor groups moved off, some of them running barefooted in single file beside their mules, their GI boots or pistol belts slung about their necks or waists, their long, curved knives hanging at their sides. By the twenty-third, the Tabor groups had surrounded the city from the north and south. Two days later, the northern group captured the suburb of Septèmes, thereby cutting off the last avenue of escape.

The German defenders inside Marseilles were being hampered by Resistance forces, who had started an uprising of their own on the twenty-first. But by the next day they were in difficult straits. Their appeals for help hastened the push by French regulars into the city.

French forces now began attacking from all sides. On the twenty-fourth, one battalion of Algerian riflemen, in an audacious move, pushed rapidly through the Madeleine and Blancarde districts, in effect cutting the city in two. The next day, in the southern sector, subjugation of the Notre Dame de la Garde area began in earnest. Two battalions of 3rd Algerian Infantry, recently arrived from fighting at Toulon, plus a detachment of Tabors, supported by tanks, slowly made their way up the hill against heavy resistance. Finally, at 10:00 A.M. on the twenty-sixth, the German garrison had had enough and hoisted the white flag of surrender. At the same time, the Tabor group in the northern suburbs was engaged in especially savage house-to-house, alley-to-alley, garden-to-garden fighting.

The navy and air force, as at Toulon, continued to fulfill their duties in exemplary fashion. On the twenty-fourth, the United States battleship *Nevada* fired 200 rounds against the offshore islands and the next day other ships shelled the harbor defenses with 354 rounds. On three successive days—the twenty-fifth, twenty-sixth, and twenty-seventh—Twelfth Air Force medium bombers and XII Tactical Air Command fighter bombers, despite heavy flak, concentrated on enemy gun positions near the dock area. Although their efforts did not force the harbor defenders to surrender, they did put most of their guns out of commission.

Throughout the battle there were acts of heroism and

chivalry on both sides. On the twenty-fifth, two wounded Germans presented themselves at a French command post.[9] They carried a message from Colonel von Hanstein, the sector commander, who said he could not take care of all of his wounded and asked that the French send an ambulance to evacuate them. The French realized Hanstein was telling the truth, for they had earlier intercepted German radio messages that indicated all of his doctors had been killed and that no more could be furnished. The French therefore agreed to provide an ambulance, which made three trips carrying twenty German wounded behind French lines to receive medical attention.

By the night of the twenty-seventh, the Germans held only the dock area, and the French were preparing for the "battle of the quays." General Schaefer, ensconced in his underground command post, finally realized the hopelessness of the situation and requested a ceasefire. At eight the next morning, General Monsabert met with Schaefer and dictated the surrender terms, putting particular emphasis on ways to prevent further destruction of the port facilities. The Germans only incompletely complied with the terms since the death of their harbormaster caused widespread confusion.[10] The result was that German engineers continued to set off demolitions and blocked portions of the harbor throughout the morning hours before the surrender took effect at 1:00 P.M. That same afternoon, 7,000 German prisoners were marched into captivity. On the twenty-ninth, the French regulars, the Resistance forces, and the citizens of Marseilles held a victory parade. Twenty-one days sooner than expected, they had opened the southern gateway into France.

The results of the battle for the ports indicated a French victory of impressive proportions. At a coast of approximately 4,000 French casualties, including 800 killed, Toulon and Marseilles had been liberated, French forces had again proved themselves in combat (taking 37,000 prisoners in the process), and Resistance fighters had demonstrated their willingness and determination to assist in evicting the enemy. The Allied naval and air arms had also contributed greatly to the outcome.

More importantly from a military standpoint, the main ports of southern France could now serve as a conduit for men and material into the interior. The goal was to use Toulon, and especially Marseilles, with excellent rail facilities to the north, not only to replenish the Dragoon froces, but eventually to help supply other Allied formations in the west as well. While Allied personnel continued the laborious task of unloading troops and cargo across the invasion beaches, American Seabees and army engineers set to work to clear the harbor areas. The damage at both ports was extensive, including approximately seventy-five sunken ships at Marseilles which blocked docks and channels. But on September 3 at Marseilles and the next day at Toulon, military and civilian laborers, including a few Vietnamese workers, began to receive supplies at some of the quays. (The first troopships were able to unload at Marseilles and Toulon on September 15 and 20 respectively.) Because of their fear that Marseilles might not be of early use, the Allies had also decided to develop Port-de-Bouc, west of Marseilles, which had served for years as a port of origin for Rhône River barge traffic, and which the Germans had evacuated on August 21. By September 2, it was open, and in the months ahead it became increasingly important as a depot for unloading and storing petroleum products. And while the early opening of Marseilles, Toulon, and Port-de-Bouc did not signal an end to Allied supply problems, it did assure that these harbors would play a continuing role in the months ahead.

While the French reduced Toulon and Marseilles, American forces fanned out along a number of axes—west through

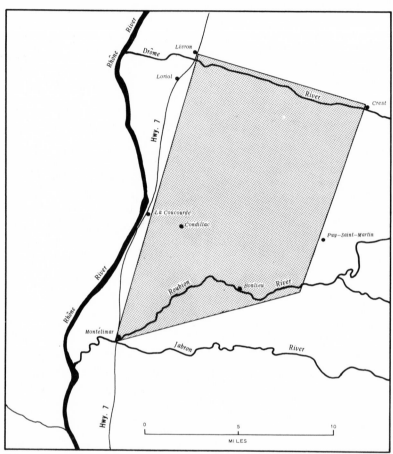

Montélimar Quadrilateral

Aix-en-Provence and toward the lower Rhône, north through Sisteron to Grenoble, and east through Cannes and Nice toward the Italian border.[11] In all instances, except for the eastern push, the Allies had two primary goals—to advance north as rapidly as possible and to capture large numbers of Wehrmacht troops in the process.

As the battle zone in southeastern France moved north, the mountains became more steep and rugged, the Provence Alps merging into the Dauphiné Alps, which stretch north and east toward the Swiss and Italian borders. The main routes north are the Grenoble corridor and the Rhône River valley. The Rhône, which flows west into Lyons, and then cuts a path straight south, 180 miles, through Avignon and Arles to the sea, is the more favored route. For between Avignon and Lyons, two main highways follow the river— Highway 7 on the east bank and the less direct Highway 86 on the west bank. Railways on both sides of the river also link the lower Rhône to French cities in the north. In addition, three major east-west rivers cut across the region and flow into the Rhone—the Durance at Avignon, the Drôme at Loriol, the Isère just north of Valence. Highways follow these rivers and smaller streams out of the Alps, and they provide the means for shifting forces laterally across the area.

The 3rd Division was assigned the task of moving west along Highway 7 toward the lower Rhône. From noon on August 19 until noon the next day, General O'Daniel's troops advanced nearly thirty miles against relatively light opposition. But then one regiment, the 30th, ran into fierce resistance as it approached Aix-en-Provence, and the city was not taken until the twenty-first. After capturing that city, the division was ordered to move northwest cautiously amid reports of a possible 11th Panzer Division counterattack. (Actually, 11th Panzer and elements of the 198th and 338th Infantry divisions were establishing a series of phase lines to cover the retreat of German forces from the area and from the Rhône triangle.) At this point the Americans inched west, making sure that French forces fighting to the south were protected, while at the same time preparing for an assault north.

Meanwhile, General Eagles's "Thunderbird" Division crossed the Durance River, swollen by mountain rains, and proceeded west to Pertuis and then north to Apt. The town, located immediately south of Petrarch's famous Mont Ventoux, was occupied on the twenty-second. The day before, the division's 179th Regiment had moved east in the opposite direction and reached Château-Arnoux, astride Highway 85, which had already been cleared by Task Force Butler on the nineteenth. This meant that 45th Division regiments were now separated from each other by as many as sixty miles.

Throughout the period, Task Force Butler had been extremely active. On the nineteenth, while the main body crossed the Durance at Oraison and made for Sisteron, two reconnaissance detachments moved east and overtook elements of the German 157th Reserve Division, capturing 500 of the enemy at Digne on the Route Napoléon. The main force reached Sisteron that afternoon and established a command post there in anticipation of continuing the advance.

At Sisteron two alternate routes lead to Grenoble—Highway 75 to the west and the Route Napoléon to the east. On the twentieth, General Butler decided to have his armored force follow Highway 75, but allowed part of the column, supported by partisans, to swing east from Aspres and seize Gap, on the eastern route. By evening, the task force controlled both Gap and the Col de la Croix Haute mountain pass to the west on Highway 75. Both were approximately fifty miles south of Grenoble.

At 8:45 P.M. General Butler received a radio message from General Truscott. "You will move at first light with all

possible speed to Montelimar. . . . Block all routes of withdrawal up the Rhone Valley in that vicinity. 36 Division follows you."[12] The following morning General Butler left several holding forces at key places and began moving his main
force west along Highway 93 and the Drôme River valley toward the Rhône.

Meanwhile, on the twentieth, the 36th Division had begun pushing north from Draguignan. At 7:00 P.M. advance
elements reached Sisteron, and on the next day General
Dahlquist's division began relieving Task Force Butler units
above Gap and at Col de la Croix Haute. Throughout this
mountainous area, the Resistance forces were of inestimable
value. An entry in the combat journal of the United States
143rd Regiment is typical of the praise they received. "In this
area, FFI forces were strong. . . . Passage through the mountain river gorges would have been impossible for our motor
convoys without the flank protection of the FFI since the
Germans, had they not been harassed by these French patri-
ots, could have sent demolitions to block the road northward
under tons of rock to hold up our motor columns for an
indefinite period."[13]

During the twenty-first, the 36th continued advancing
north toward Grenoble. That evening, a message was received from General Truscott, directing one regiment, with
attached artillery, to head west and reinforce Task Force Butler in its drive to the Rhône. Although the 141st Regiment,
which was given the assignment, had difficulties obtaining
gasoline from the beaches, one battalion started moving out
on the twenty-second, and the rest followed suit early the
next morning. That same night, the 142nd Regiment, which
was located east of Gap, was also ordered to head west. On
the twenty-third it began to pull out, following the 141st.
While these two regiments moved west, the 143rd Regiment
(less one battalion) was closing in on Grenoble. After some

bitter fighting in front of the city, on the morning of the twenty-second, the Americans along with French partisans and paratroopers, entered Grenoble without opposition. (German resistance in the area had generally been light because the 157th Division was unable to cover adequately both the deep flank in the mountains east of the Grenoble corridor and the city itself.) The next day, the United States 143rd Regiment was relieved by elements of the 45th Division, and it hurried west to join the other "Texas" Division formations immediately east of the Rhône. The battle of Montélimar, the heaviest fighting in the Allied northerly advance, was already beginning to unfold.

The eight-day battle took place in a quadrilateral northeast of the road and rail center of Montélimar.[14] The quadrilateral runs roughly fifteen miles north-south by ten miles east-west, with the towns of Montélimar, Livron, Crest, and Charois at the corners of the battle area. The Rhône, which formed the western side of the quadrilateral, is relatively narrow between Montélimar and Livron and characterized by a deep gorge with steep banks on both sides. Immediately east and parallel to the river are a railway and Highway 7, the main escape routes north. Farther east is the Marsanne forest, whose heights overlook the highway and the town of Montélimar itself.

The Drôme River, the northern boundary of the so-called "battle square," widens into a two-mile valley at Crest and then flows west and empties into the Rhône near Loriol. Control of its bridges and fording places would also prevent an enemy from moving north. The eastern side of the quadrilateral is the only portion not bounded by a river, but it has several secondary roads, D6 and 538, between Puy-Saint-Martin and Crest, which could be used for military traffic or supplies. The southern side generally follows road D6 and the Roubion River southwest from Puy-Saint-Martin and

Charois to Montélimar. The force which controlled this southern corridor was in a favorable position to block any traffic moving east of Montélimar. Hills to the east of the battle area prevented any large-scale movement north. To the west, several bridges cross the Rhône west of Montélimar and Loriol, and the enemy might use them to get to the more circuitous but still passable Highway 86 on the western bank.

Advance elements of Task Force Butler reached Crest, the northeast corner of the quadrilateral, during the day of August 21. As the task force followed the Drôme River valley toward the Rhône, it came upon an enemy column of about thirty vehicles moving north on Highway 7. The task force attacked and destroyed the vehicles, killing and wounding a number of the enemy. Among the prisoners were eleven Russian workers from a labor battalion. That night patrols were sent out to cut Highway 7 farther south, but they were driven back by enemy troops. This action only sustained the Allies' original belief that Butler's armored column alone would be insufficient. It was also obvious to General Truscott that the Germans, though not yet in the area in strength, intended to use the Rhône valley as the major route for their retreat.

The VI Corps commander's call for 36th Division reinforcements had gone out on the evening of the twenty-first. The next morning, the hard-driving Truscott went to Dahlquist's command post to follow up on his orders. A little later he sent a scathing letter to the 36th Division commander. "I visited your command Post this morning and, as your Chief of Staff has probably informed you, was considerably upset because my original instruction covered in subsequent messages has not been carried out. Apparently, I failed to make your mission clear to you. The primary mission of the 36th ID is to block the Rhone Valley in the gap immediately north of Montelimar. For this purpose you must be prepared to employ the bulk of your division."[15] As alluded to earlier, General Dahlquist was having difficulties getting the necessary gasoline to transport his troops, located eighty miles to the west, to the battle area. Later on the twenty-second, he relayed to Truscott a message outlining his proposed course of action and added the following personal note. "There is absolutely no gas available at the beaches. I have less than 5,000 gallons. Be assured I realize the situation and I am dispatching forces to Butler to the maximum extent allowable by transport."[16]

The exchange was not over. At 8:55 P.M., Truscott repeated to Dahlquist by telephone the urgency of his orders. "Your primary mission is to block the Rhone Valley and I expect you to do it. . . . And when you run out of gas you park your trucks and move on foot." Still not satisfied, Truscott made another phone call to the 36th Division at 2:00 A.M. on the twenty-third. "I want to get word to Butler or to General Dahlquist, if he is over there, to interrupt by demolitions that main road on the Rhone Valley. I don't want a single vehicle to go up that road."

By this time, portions of Dahlquist's 141st Regiment were entering the battle zone. They moved south from Crest and established a command post at Condillac, along a narrow pass, six miles northeast of Montélimar. Several miles to the west is the town of La Coucourde and the east bank of the Rhône. By 1:00 P.M., all of the regiment had reached the area, and that afternoon one battalion launched an attack toward Montélimar, but was repulsed by enemy artillery fire. Unable to seize Montélimar, the 141st had to content itself with attempting to control the hills north of town and east of Highway 7.

For the Allies, the battle was already evolving into an attempt to bring sufficient troops and firepower to bear on the enemy so as to prevent his withdrawal. This was not always easy to accomplish. Supplies were generally coming from the invasion beaches to the battle area by way of Aspres in the Grenoble corridor, a one-way distance of 235 miles. At times the Germans were able to cut off this main supply route through Crest, and alternative routes had to be devised. To the south, where the distances were not so great, the 3rd Division, which advanced to Avignon on the twenty-fifth, still had to share its allotments with the heavily engaged French forces before Toulon and Marseilles. The result was that the Americans were often short of gasoline and especially ammunition at crucial times during the fighting. From the German standpoint, their survival depended at all cost on forcing their way through the traps that were being laid for them.

By the twenty-fourth, the southern trap was set. Task Force Butler, before being placed in reserve at Puy-Saint-Martin, had put an artillery battery at Condillac pass, and other batteries were also moved into position to fire on the main highway. This forced the Germans, with the bulk of their forces immediately south of Montélimar, to seek additional escape routes east of the town. However, the Americans had anticipated the German move, and had positioned the entire 142nd Regiment, one battalion of the 141st Regiment, several smaller units, and numerous artillery battalions in a defense line along the Roubion River.

The German Nineteenth Army at this point was fighting for its life. Three divisions—the 198th Infantry, 338th Infantry, and 11th Panzer—were entrusted with holding off the United States 3rd Division to the south while opening the way for the withdrawal north.[17] To achieve the latter, portions of the 198th and 11th Panzer, including Panther tanks, fought their way east along the Roubion defense line. Having captured an American field order, the Germans realized that the village of Bonlieu, seven miles east of Montélimar, was a key point, for it formed the defensive hinge between the United States 141st and 142nd regiments. When the Germans reached Bonlieu on the afternoon of the twenty-fifth, they struck north. After two assaults they breached the American line, and Wehrmacht troops and equipment began pouring through the gap. By the time it was finally closed on the twenty-seventh, a substantial number of Germans had been able to escape north toward the Drôme River.

Also on the twenty-fifth, elements of the 11th Panzer succeeded in taking La Coucourde and gaining partial control of the hills east of Highway 7. For the next several days, Task Force Butler and the 141st Regiment made a number of attempts to establish roadblocks along the highway, but they were unable to do so for extended periods of time. Large numbers of German soldiers were thus able to make their way north, though at times being subjected to devastating artillery fire. When the gunfire became too intense, the Germans rerouted their columns west across the Rhône bridges (usually at night) to Highway 86. Although French Resistance forces were strong in this area, it was certainly less hazardous than facing American artillery barrages and fighter aircraft strafing attacks on the eastern side of the river.

On the morning of the twenty-sixth, with the Germans streaming north in three places, General Truscott visited General Dahlquist's headquarters, now located south of Crest. Truscott made no attempt to hide his displeasure with the turn of events. He later wrote:

> John, I have come here with the full intention of relieving you from your command. You have reported to me that you held the high ground north of Montelimar and that you had blocked Highway 7. You have not done so. You have failed to carry out my orders. You have just five minutes in which to convince me that you are not at fault.

Dahlquist said he had believed, from reports sent to him

that his troops were on the hills along Highway 7 north of Montelimar. He had not discovered the error until the day after, when he visited the regiment and found them on the hill east of the ridge in dispute. He had during the preceding day bent every effort to make the block effective, but the enemy had been too strong. He had been threatened by an enemy attack east from Loriol in the direction of Crest which had actually cut his supply road south of Crest, and by a strong armored attack north from Puy St. Martin toward Crest. Nevertheless, he now had a block at Coucourde [by this time removed] and had four battalions of artillery emplaced where they could interrupt the road. Except for his initial mistake, Dahlquist thought he had done as well as could be expected. I did not fully concur, but I decided against relieving him.[18]

Dahlquist, who later served in a number of important command positions before retiring from the military in 1955, admitted in a letter to his wife on the twenty-ninth: "I have a very classic military role and a great opportunity. I feel I fumbled it badly and should have done a great deal better. For seven days and nights it was a terrible strain. Strenuous fighting never developed except in small spots but one afternoon I was fighting on three sides which kind of kept me hopping. The hardest part of the strain is the necessity for resisting the desire to help everyone who asks for it."[19]

The Americans made one final attempt to trap the German forces before they could escape north. It look place along the Drôme River, the northern border of the quadrilateral. The plan was for the 36th Division's 143rd Regiment, the 45th Division's 157th Regiment, and Task Force Butler to clear the valley west from Crest and keep the enemy from crossing the river. Between August 26 and 28 the Americans made valiant efforts, with the aid of artillery and air power, to close off the lines of retreat, but the Germans would not let it happen. Using a road bridge, a railway bridge, and four fording sites near Highway 7, most of their formations were able to withdraw north before the Americans succeeded in capturing Livron on the twenty-eighth and Loriol on the twenty-ninth. The last attempt, like the first farther south, had ended in failure.

In an anticlimax, on the twenty-eighth, the 141st Regiment finally gained full control of the heights north of Montélimar. Three days earlier, the 3rd Division had been relieved by the 2nd French Combat Command at Avignon and had fought its way north. It now entered Montélimar from the south and began mopping up operations. The battle was over.

For the Allies, the battle for the Montélimar quadrilateral was at best a partial success. On the credit side, the operation had yielded a good deal of German equipment either captured or destroyed, equipment which was forever lost to the enemy and becoming increasingly difficult for him to replace. Along Highway 7 alone, as a result of artillery fire and aerial strafing attacks, the Americans counted Wehrmacht losses of approximately 2,000 motor vehicles, 1,000 horses, five railway guns, and forty other pieces of ordnance. On the debit side, United States forces had failed to block the German retreat, and most of the enemy troops had escaped north to fight another day. General Truscott's assessment after the war was probably close to the mark when he wrote, "Even if Montelimar had not been a perfect battle, we could still view the record with some degree of satisfaction."[20]

Besides the American fighting near Montélimar and the French reduction of Toulon and Marseilles, several other important developments were occurring on the flanks. On August 18, German soldiers and associated personnel west of the Rhône began pulling out and streaming north (except for those manning the Bay of Biscay "fortresses" and some troops along the border who managed to escape southward into Spain). The retreating Wehrmacht formations generally remained west of the river in their flight north and withdrew by any means available—by train, motor vehicle, bicycle, even on foot.[21] They received considerable "assistance" in their exodus from the Resistance forces, who occupied the towns as the Germans left, attacked their columns, and captured a number of prisoners. The *maquis* were particularly harsh on their fellow French citizens who had collaborated with the Germans, imprisoning, maiming, and even killing many of them. Nevertheless, by early September, most of the German units had successfully extricated themselves from southwestern France, leaving the FFI in virtual control.

On the eastern flank, by August 20, United States airborne troops had relieved the 36th Division. For the next few days, they, along with the Special Service Force, which had originally captured the offshore islands of Levant and Port-Cros, extended their defensive line northward. At the same time, reports of two enemy divisions moving west from Italy led to a decision by the Americans to improve their defensive positions by pushing east. The immediate goal was to take Cannes, along the coast, and Grasse, eleven miles inland. After engaging in a number of skirmishes, and with the assistance of naval gunfire, the paratroopers and commandos occupied the two towns on the twenty-fourth. The German 148th Division, which had received conflicting orders from Nineteenth Army to resist and from the Wehrmacht command in Italy to pull back, decided to abandon the towns (with active assistance from the Resistance) even before the Americans arrived.[22] The theater history briefly describes the entrance into Cannes as follows, "The 509th Parachute Infantry Battalion, crowded on tank destroyers, rode into

Cannes, The streets were lined with wildly cheering people. Some were 'crying openly.' Others threw flowers into passing American vehicles."[23]

During the next week, the United States forces continued their eastward advance, taking Nice—in part for psychological reasons, in part because of its harbor facilities—on the thirtieth. By September 8, the entire French Mediterranean coast was in Allied hands. With the bulk of the forces streaming north, the Americans assumed a defensive posture near the Italian border. Farther north, where the mountainous terrain played a role, elements of the 45th Division held the area east of Grenoble, until August 28, when they were relieved by a composite American force under Lt. Col. Harold S. Bibo, a War Department observer with the Seventh Army.[24] Five days later, Colonel Bibo's mixed unit of cavalry, chemical, antitank, and artillery troops was relieved by regular formations from French Army B.

Just as the situation on the flanks changed dramatically during the last ten days of August, so did the situation for the Allied air and naval forces. Originally, XII Tactical Air Command and carrier aircraft had concentrated on attacking fixed defenses, such as gun positions, and the enemy transportation network.[25] But the rapid push north and west forced them to modify their thinking. General Saville's fighters and Twelfth Air Force medium bombers still struck at German fortifications, as at Toulon and Marseilles, but air leaders found that severing road and rail lines might be more of a disadvantage than an advantage because of the Allies' rapid northerly advance. This led to an increased emphasis on attempting to block enemy escape routes and on close tactical air support rather than concentrating on logistics targets. However, the air support missions were especially difficult to carry out in the Montélimar quadrilateral, where the interpenetration of the two sides made them virtually impossible, and Allied pilots turned increasingly to hitting targets west of the Rhône and north of the Drôme River. Nonetheless, between August 21 and 28, the Allies flew 3,299 sorties in the XII Tactical Air Command area and dropped 1,907 tons of bombs.

The movement away from the coast also caused several other alterations for the air component. Allied planners had long realized the need for airfields on the mainland, and this need now became even more imperative with the movement inland. By August 24, Allied engineers had six airfields in service, but the fighters (mainly P-47s and Spitfires) operating from them were still unable to keep sufficient pressure on the retreating enemy. And with the closing down of Toulon, Marseilles, and Montélimar operations, the enemy was beyond carrier plane range, so the task force was transferred out of the area for other missions.

The navy reorganized its other forces, too.[26] Many of the gunfire support ships sailed away, and the coast placed under the protection of one battleship (the French *Lorraine*), six cruisers, eight destroyers, and other smaller craft. The navy now turned its attention to clearing the central Mediterranean of remaining enemy vessels. On September 4, heavy bombers dropped 491 tons of bombs on the Genoa dock area, and this air raid virtually eliminated the German navy. Except for some small ships along the Italian coast, German naval activity (including that of U-boats) was no longer a factor in the western Mediterranean.

Two weeks after the invasion, Allied commanders could indeed be pleased with the results. Three hundred and eighty miles of French Mediterranean coastline had been liberated and the major ports cleared of the enemy. American forces, with substantial help from the Resistance, stood at Grenoble, 200 miles inland by road from the coast, and at Livron, 100 miles up the Rhône. The FFI was in the final stages of taking over the area west of the river. In short, most of southern France was now in Allied hands.

The casualties had been much lower than anticipated—through August 24, 6,337 Americans (including 1,247 killed and missing), 3,179 French, and 297 British, 9,813 in all.[27] Some 50,000 prisoners had been taken, and a prisoner of war hospital staffed by captured German medical teams was to be established in the area. Also the number of troops and the amount of cargo unloaded across the beaches had reached 190,565 personnel, 41,536 vehicles, and 219,205 tons of supplies. This amount would increase even more with the opening of Port-de-Bouc, Marseilles, and Toulon in the near future. A report from Field Marshal Wilson to the British Chiefs of Staff ably summarized the campaign to date. "Thanks to the skill with which it was mounted and carried through by all three Services, Operation Dragoon has been an outstanding success."

Whether the early momentum could be sustained was another matter. The victory had been achieved so quickly that it was difficult for the Allies to consider any alternatives besides the one being pursued. As long as supplies were forthcoming, the main goals therefore continued to be tactical rather than strategic—to chase the retreating enemy, to hope to cut him off before he could establish an effective defensive line, and to effect a junction with Patton's Third Army, now advancing rapidly across central France. General Devers, trying hard to restrain himself, but anxious to join the fray, suggested that the United States Fifth Army be removed from Italy "by all manner of craft to south France," but his suggestion was resisted by Wilson and turned aside at the Quebec Conference in September.[28] Italy, already starved for troops, was not to be denuded of American ground forces.

On August 29, the major Allied commanders in the Mediterranean met at Seventh Army headquarters at Brignoles.[29]

Although there was some discussion about the timing involved in transferring Patch's forces from the Mediterranean to Eisenhower's European command, the main portion of the meeting was devoted to what was to happen next. General Patch indicated that his tactical plan (Field Order No. 4) called for more of the same: the Seventh Army was to continue its advance north; VI Corps was to spearhead the attack with American forces converging on Lyons from the south and east and then pushing on toward Dijon, 130 miles to the north. On the left, part of de Lattre's French Army B was to move along the west bank of the Rhône and assist in the capture of Lyons. On the right, other portions of French Army B were to advance north behind the Americans and then slip east around the Swiss border in the direction of Besançon. They were also to relieve VI Corps units guarding the mountain passes east of Grenoble and north of Larche. General Frederick's 1st Airborne Task Force was to continue protecting the flank south of Larche and immediately west of the Italian border.

By the time the conference had ended, the chase was already underway.[30] On the twenty-seventh and twenty-eighth, two regiments of the 45th Division pushed northwest from Grenoble and advance elements reached Bourgoin the next day. On the thirtieth, most of Task Force Butler merged into the 45th, and the "Thunderbird" Division continued its northerly drive. By the thirty-first, it had crossed the Rhône between Lyons and the Swiss boundary and arrived at Meximieux, twenty miles east of Lyons. A day earlier the 36th Division had started moving north along the Rhône, occupied Valence without a fight, and crossed the Isère River on the thirty-first. At the same time, the 3rd Division, having cleared Montélimar, headed north to reassemble at Voiron so as to be in position to assist the 45th Division in its dash north. At this stage advances of from twenty to thirty miles per day became common with reconnaissance elements in the lead, followed by infantry riding on tanks and tank destroyers, in two-and-one-half-ton trucks, and on artillery and weapons vehicles bringing up the rear. General Dahlquist, in a letter to his wife on the thirtieth, verified that the pace was exhausing. "Everyone is tired. We have been going at a terrific pace with practically no chance to rest. This afternoon I fell sound asleep in my jeep. However, we cannot stop and much as I dislike it I have to keep driving. It looks as though we still have a lot to do before we can rest."[31] By the second, stiff enemy resistance at Meximieux led the 45th Division to bypass the town and to head toward Bourg-en-Bresse. The task of capturing Meximieux was left to General O'Daniel's 3rd Division. In the meantime, the 36th had pressed forward to the southern outskirts of Lyons.

In spite of the swift American advance, few Germans were caught in the onrush.[32] Gen. Baptist Kniess, commander of the LXXV Corps, managed to set up two defensive screens—elements of the 198th and 338th Infantry Division with thirty-four artillery pieces and three antitank guns to the south of Lyons, and the 11th Panzer with twelve tanks, seven assault guns, and fourteen antitank weapons to the east. These forces effectively covered the withdrawal—at times putting up stout resistance, at times disengaging when faced by intense Allied pressure—but almost always keeping some distance between their large number of retreating troops and the Americans.

To the left of the United States forces, General du Vigier had assumed command of the 1st French and 1st Armored divisions, which were to lead the push north along the western side of the Rhône. On the thirtieth, while portions of du Vigier's force reconnoitered southwest into the area liberated by the Resistance, the bulk of his two divisions moved rapidly toward Lyons. Though hampered by a lack of fuel and truck transport, by the second, they were closing in on the city. (That same day the two divisions became part of the II Corps under General Monsabert.)

The Americans, following the recent precedents at Paris and elsewhere, allowed the French the honor of taking this famous center of France's silk industry. Through the day, the 1st Division, with the help of the *maquis*, invested Lyons from the west and northwest. At the same time, the 1st Armored Division formed a screening force farther west and cut the Saône River bridges to the north. The next morning, finding the Germans had pulled out, the French, with Bayard's Resistance group leading the way, entered Lyons. Scenes such as this could not help but evoke a flood of emotion, and many soldiers shared General de Lattre's sentiment, "How wonderful it was to be in France again."[33]

On the extreme right of the battle area, three divisions of French Army B began heading north from the coast toward Grenoble. The recently landed 2nd Moroccan Division took over defense of the Alpine passes near the Italian border. The 3rd Algerian Division relieved the last elements of the United States 45th Division at Grenoble and undertook its own movement north to assume the offensive. The 9th Colonial, still detained by garrison duties at Toulon, was to follow later. On September 2, orders were sent out that the three divisions would now form the French I Corps with General Béthouart, being recalled from Italy, as its commander. By the next day, the 3rd Algerian, which had recently distinguished itself at Toulon and Marseilles, was in position beside the Americans and ready to join the chase.

Allied advances of this magnitude were bound to exact their toll. For one thing, the troops were exhausted. On the third, for example, two companies of the highly regarded United States 117th Cavalry Squadron went to sleep and were surrounded and captured.[34] (It was latter learned the companies had gone around the rear of the German 11th Panzer Division during the day. That night, when the 11th Panzer withdrew, it came upon the Americans, surprised them, and overran their positions.)

Just as importantly, XII Tactical Air Command was having difficulties keeping pace with the advance.[35] By September 3, General Saville had fighter groups (but no bombs) located at airfields as far north as Montélimar, Valence, and Sisteron. The old bases near the coast were too far back to base fighter aircraft, especially with their need for more loitering time to strike at targets of opportunity. This factor, combined with the return of medium bombers and Corsica-based aircraft to the battle in Italy, resulted in XII Tactical Air Command flying only 1,303 sorties and dropping a mere fifty tons of bombs between August 29 and September 4, as compared with 3,299 sorties and 1,907 tons the week before. With the liberation of Lyons, the situation was expected to improve, but for the moment, the amount of close air support that could be provided was substantially reduced.

Another problem was the growing fear among Allied Commanders that they were outrunning their supplies. On the whole, supply units had done a remarkable job, even enlisting injured troops who had difficulty walking but who still could drive trucks.[36] Nevertheless, supply lines from the beaches were becoming increasingly stretched, the ports were only just beginning to come into use, and the amount of railway rolling stock and engineering bridging equipment was insufficient at this point to support large numbers of troops. Then there was the matter of gasoline. Clearly the chase could be sustained only if this vital commodity, already in short supply, were ready and available.

Nevertheless, the capture of Lyons and the American thrust east of the city seemed to provide the Allies with a final opportunity to cut off the Germans before they could escape behind a defensive line in eastern France. (The Germans were also fully aware of the possibility and had moved Army Task Force G headquarters to Dijon as early as August 24.) On September 2, General Truscott pressed General Patch to adopt a bold course of action rather than, as originally planned, regrouping the Dragoon forces once Lyons had been taken.[37] While Patch realized that there was only a "fleeting opportunity," he was willing to take the chance. The regrouping would take place later.

Instead of moving all of the French forces to the right near the Swiss border (except for those guarding the Italian frontier), they were to remain split into two groups. General Monsabert's II Corps was to advance north from Lyons to Chalon-sur-Saône and Dijon and link up with elements of Patton's Third Army. On the right, General Béthouart's I Corps was to move through the Jura Alps along the Swiss boundary and swing north in an attempt to reach Belfort before the bulk of the Wehrmacht forces could get there. In the middle, Truscott's VI Corps was given the same objective—to arrive at the Belfort Gap, the gateway to the Upper Rhine, before the Germans—but it was to be by way of Highway 83, the city of Besançon, and the Doubs River. Patch's order, in essence, was designated to turn the chase into a race for the Belfort Gap. The Allied prize, if successful, would be large numbers of German prisoners, a prize which had eluded them thus far.

As early as September 3, the 3rd Algerian Division on the right was registering spectacular gains. It slipped east against slight opposition and moved with great speed more than 140 miles, arriving at Pontarlier near the Swiss border the next evening. (General de Lattre records with some satisfaction that at this time the United States 45th Division, the spearhead of the VI Corps attack, was still assembling at Bourg-en-Bresse, far to the rear.)[38] On the fifth, after capturing

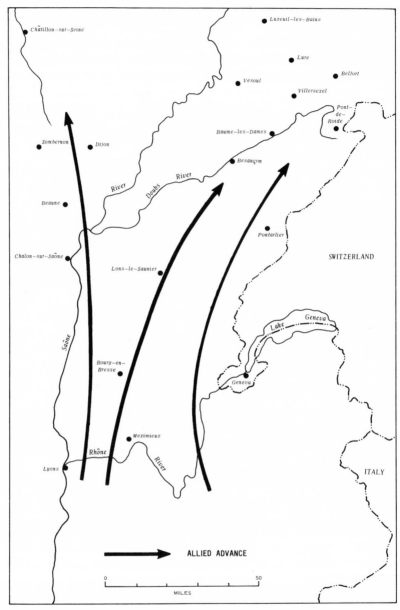

Race for the Belfort Gap

Pontarlier, the French advance continued, but the French then began to run into stiff resistance from the German 11th Panzer. On the eighth, after probing north and east, the 3rd Algerian Division pushed to near Pont-de-Roide, only thirty miles south of Belfort. However, they were now stopped and unable to advance further.

In the meantime, the resupplied United States divisions had started their advance northeast along Highway 83. On September 5, the "Thunderbird" Division passed through Lons-le-Saunier and headed for Besançon, fifty miles away, but turned northeast before reaching the heavily fortified city. On the seventh, using footbridges, improvised barges, and a local ferry because the bridges had been blown, they crossed the Doubs River east of Besançon and attacked the town of Baume-les-Dames. The offensive now showed signs of slowing, for Baume-les-Dames was not taken until the ninth after heavy fighting.

The United States 3rd Division followed behind the 45th and closed in on Besançon from the south.[39] Elements of the 36th Division, which had cleared Dole, arrived from the west to lend a hand. Besançon, which lies astride the Doubs, was defended by soldiers in five forts, including one designed by the famous seventeenth-century engineer, Vauban, and was considered difficult to penetrate. The Americans proceeded to surround the city from three sides. The Seventh Army history describes part of the action.

A battalion of the 30th Infantry [Regiment] crossed the swamp-lands northeast of Besancon and occupied the village and fort at Montfaucon. From this elevation tanks, tank destroyers, and artillery fired at enemy vehicles withdrawing along the Belfort Road. "I never saw such confusion in my life," reported a tank destroyer commander. "Germans were flying every way, ammunition going off and flares lit the place like the Fourth of July back home." The enemy continued to withdraw from the city, but left behind delaying forces of infantry armed with machine guns and mortars.

On the seventh, the forts were taken one after another, and the next day Besançon fell to the Americans. In addition to 653 prisoners, a fuel dump with 177,500 gallons of usable gasoline and 4,000 gallons of alcohol was captured before it could be set ablaze.

While United States forces reduced Besançon, the French II Corps on the left moved north of Lyons along the Saône River. Though unable to bag many of the enemy battle groups still withdrawing to the east, General du Vigier's 1st Armored and Brosset's 1st French divisions continued their advance, taking Chalon-sur-Saône on the sixth and Beaune on the eighth. Only twenty-five miles farther was Dijon, the traditional capital of Burgundy, on one of the last remaining escape routes open to the Wehrmacht. When several German counterattacks in front of Dijon failed to halt the French, the former elected not to defend the city, and the 1st Armored Division occupied it undamaged on the tenth.

The French were well aware that elements of Patton's Third Army were driving south to link up with their Dragoon forces, and they set out to effect the junction. On the night of September 10–11, at Sombernon, west of Dijon, one of du Vigier's patrols made contact with a small reconnaissance group of General Le Clerc's 2nd French Armored Division, which was attached to Patton's army.[40] At 7:00 A.M. on the twelfth, reconnaissance troops of the 1st French Division met Le Clerc's division near Châtillon on the Seine River, halfway between Dijon and Troyes, and the permanent link between north and south was now forged. This constituted the second such honor the 2nd Armored had participated in in less than three weeks. On August 25, they had led the march into Paris. In a related action, on the same day that French forces joined near Châtillon, 18,000 Wehrmacht personnel, including two generals and one admiral, surrendered to French soldiers west of the Saône River. Except for the Bay of Biscay fortresses, southwestern France was now completely cleared of enemey troops.

To the east, American and French forces had continued their drive toward the Belfort Gap. The French I Corps had to content itself with small gains near Pont-de-Roide, but the United States 45th Division, on September 10, sped north as far as Villersexel, only twenty miles west of Belfort. However, at this point German opposition once again stiffened. For three days and nights bitter fighting ensued. The 45th Division's 2nd Lt. Almond E. Fisher won a Medal of Honor for his heroism. The citation read in part as follows, "Wounded in both feet, he eliminated four machine gun emplacements alone, then refusing to be evacuated, directed his platoon in a successful defense against a savage counterattack."[41]

The reason for the enemy's determined resistance was described after the war by Gen. Walter Botsch, who served as chief of staff for Nineteenth Army and was heavily involved in the retreat.

> The thrust of the 45th US Div north from Baume les Dames on Villersexel was the most dangerous and most critical potentially for us of all the different attacks launched by the French and the Americans at this time in that region. 11 Panzer was tied down between the Doubs and the Swiss frontier to protect Belfort. The bulk of the IV Air Force Field Corps and the LXIV Army Corps [originally west of the Rhône] were still far to the west in order to steer German forces coming from southern France and to keep open a concentrated area for German armored forces. The thrust of the 45th US Div was aimed at the backs of the LXIV Corps and the IV Air Force Field Corps. Against this it was possible to engage only quickly scraped together units, the Dehner battle group. However, this group, assisted by elements of the 11 Panzer Division, succeeded in parrying this dangerous thrust.[42]

The 45th did not take Villersexel until the thirteenth.

During this time, the other two American divisions, the 3rd and 36th, had continued their drive northeast after capturing Besançon. At this stage they were helped a good deal by XII Tactical Air Command fighters and fighter bombers, now operating from airfields close to Lyons. They also benefited from receiving additional supplies and gasoline, which were being airlifted (in some cases by B-24s) to nearby airfields and then transported to them by truck.[43] On the eleventh, the United States divisions reached the road and rail hub of Vesoul, thirty-two miles west of Belfort. The Germans did not make as determined a stand to defend the city as expected, capitulating on the thirteenth. The Americans kept pushing, and took Luxeuil and Lure on the northern flank on the sixteenth.

However, all along the front it was becoming evident that the enemy was no longer withdrawing rapidly and was digging in to fight. The Allies were well aware of why the Germans were no longer retreating.[44] They were now in contact and linked with Army Group B on their right. They were in positions just west of the north-south defensive line that German engineers were preparing from Belfort north along the Vosges Mountains and the Moselle River. Their supply lines had grown shorter, and reinforcements were being brought in. Resistance and Allied air activity had decreased considerably in recent days. What the Allies did not appreciate at the time was that General Blaskowitz's Army Task Force G (it had been upgraded to an army group on September 10) had just executed a retreat of almost incredible proportions. The withdrawal had covered more than 400 miles (in some instances substantially more) over a period of twenty-eight days. As a result of their feat, German soldiers could now turn around and engage their adversaries from more favorable, conventional defensive positions.

On the fourteenth, an Allied order to their units to re-group, in effect, acknowledged their failure to win the race for Belfort. On the next day, as already planned, overall control passed from Wilson's Mediterranean to Eisenhower's European command. Tactically, instead of being under General Patch's guidance, General Devers took over as head of Sixth Army Group, which now became operational with its head-quarters at Lyons. (Patch actually continued to direct operations for the next several days to ease the transition.) All of de Lattre's French Army B (soon to be redesignated the more appropriate First French Army) was to move to the right flank in front of Belfort (except for the division protecting the Italian frontier).[45] Patch's Seventh Army, besides guarding the Franco-Italian border south of Larche, was to reorganize its three VI Corps divisions for a northeasterly thrust toward Strasbourg. General Truscott argued vehemently against the order, preferring to send his formations directly east against Belfort. But after several heated exchanges between him and General Patch, in which Truscott at one point said, "If you think someone else can do this job better than I, it is all right with me," the VI Corps commander, who was later to serve with equally great distinction as head of Fifth Army in Italy, gave in to Patch's plan. Amidst all of the reorganizing, one point was clear: the Dragoon phase had come to an end; a broader phase (both in terms of area and duration)—the attempt to drive into Hitler's Germany—was about to begin.

Between September 3 and 15, the twelve days between the capture of Lyons and the halt before Belfort, American and French forces had gained some successes and suffered some failures. Large amounts of territory—it is approximately 200 miles from Lyons, and 120 miles from Dijon, to Belfort—had been overrun and cleared of the enemy. Though not as many as hoped, nearly 30,000 prisoners had been added to the roll of captured German troops. Allied groups of armies in northern and southern France had been joined into a single front. Because of the rapid advance, demolitions had been less than expected, and supplies, while often stretched to the limit, had seldom broken down in spite of the great distance involved. (General Devers considered Generals Thomas Larkin and Arthur Wilson, who directed the supply effort, to be logistics geniuses.)[46] While the Resistance was not as strong in this area and its direct role decreased to an extent, this was more than offset by the 40,000 Frenchmen who swelled the ranks of the regular army as it moved north. General Dahlquist's letter of September 5 to his wife is perhaps indicative of the general atmosphere which prevailed in the French countryside during this period. "I am still enchanted by the country. It is beyond my description . . . [and] the people are simply delirious with joy at our coming. Today I saw hundreds of them standing on the roadside trying to give eggs, pears, apples, bread, wine to our soldiers. Sometimes they throw fruit at us and when one is traveling 40 miles an hour a pear or a tomato in the face is rather disastrous."[47]

To be sure, as the front lengthened into eastern France, problems did ensue. When the Allies approached the neutral Swiss border, the Swiss called up their forces just in case.[48] At times they turned their backs as the number of Allied repatriates (including downed pilots) illegally crossing the frontier increased dramatically. But at times incidents broke out which had to be quelled. They were especially upset by Allied intrusions into Swiss airspace. On September 11 alone, the Swiss reported thirty such violations, including an attack by two United States P-47 Thunderbolts against an express train traveling from Zurich to Basel which resulted in several injuries. American diplomats apologized profusely to Swiss officials and tried to assure them that similar incidents would not recur (of course, some did before the end of the war).

The conduct of American soldiers was not always above reproach, either.[49] The number of desertions, which usually took place among infantry troops near the front lines, was relatively low. But United States troops could not always be restrained from "helping themselves" from houses along the way. At the village of Bonnal, for instance, they looted the house of a respected inhabitant, Pujet, stealing some silver-plated eggs and all the provisions which were to be used in the forthcoming marriage of his daughter. Near the same village, a farm family named Vaspard had all of their goods and some of their clothing carried off. While the French said they did not begrudge the Americans wine and spirits and food, in spite of their own hardships, they begged United States officials to see that the taking of irreplaceable items cease. At the same time, American military leaders tried to keep their forces in the rear areas in line by placing Cannes, Nice, and Monaco, "those notorious hotbeds of intrigue and espionage," off limits. According to General Patch, for the time being, United States personnel should go outside southern France for their recreation and rest.

On September 15, the Allies' pursuit of German forces to the foothills before Belfort came to an end. In a sense, the Allies had lost the race, failing to capture large numbers of enemy troops. But in another sense, they had during the nearly month-long chase registered notable triumphs. The seizure of Toulon and Marseilles ahead of schedule; the taking of Grenoble, Lyons, Dijon, and Besançon; the opening of the Rhône transportation artery into central France; the liberation of all of southern France (except for two Atlantic ports), these were distinct accomplishments.

Overall, after thirty days of fighting, the statistics of the

Dragoon operation showed a maximum Allied effort and minimum losses.[50] Unloading figures indicate that 263,476 personnel, 56,318 vehicles, and 526,039 tons of cargo had been landed through mid-September. Moreover, with Toulon, Marseilles, and Port-de-Bouc now coming on line, the beach entrepôts could be shut down. On September 9, Alpha beaches were closed, followed by Delta on the sixteenth and Camel on the twenty-fifth.

During the month, the number of prisoners captured totaled nearly 79,000. Casualty figures, while always elusive, numbered approximately 13,208, including 7,419 Americans (3,000 killed), 5,492 French (1,146 killed), and 297 British (156 killed and missing). In the air and sea operations, Mediterranean air forces flew 23,808 Dragoon-related sorties and dropped 14,030 tons of bombs between August 10 and September 11. The navy's huge Western Task Force through September 25 listed only thirteen ships lost and forty-seven damaged. The numbers given above obviously go a long way to support the conclusion that the French Riviera campaign was an outstanding tactical success for the Allies. Whether it was a strategic success as well will be examined in the chapter that follows.

6

An Assessment

BEFORE DISCUSSING the French Riviera campaign from a strategic standpoint, it would be helpful to set forth once again the main reasons for its tactical success. One reason was that the Allied forces faced a weakened, and on the whole, dispirited foe. In spite of Germany's foreknowledge as to the time and the approximate location of the attack, by August 15 there was little Army Task Force G could do to turn back a full-scale assault. Their best formations (as well as equipment) had been sent north. Their coastal artillery batteries were of little immediate assistance, since the Americans, as in other instances, elected not to attack the major ports frontally. And the German navy and air force were barely capable of handling normal patrol duties, let alone repelling an Allied invasion in force.

Another reason for Dragoon's success was that it was an exceedingly well-planned, well-coordinated operation carried out by experienced commanders and staffs. Detailed planning for an assault against southern France began as early as January 1944, and one might contend even earlier. American, French, and British planners undertook an extensive examination of the enemy's defense system and of the terrain and approaches involved.[1] As early as March 1944 they decided that the attack should take place on the French Riviera coast between Cavalaire-sur-Mer and Agay and made their plans accordingly. The major problems which remained for them were the uncertainty of whether Anvil (and later Dragoon) would ever be launched at all and the late date at which the actual size of the forces was agreed upon. But even these problems were not insuperable, for the Allies, with a good deal of experience in mounting amphibious operations behind them, possessed the know-how and flexibility to deal with the variety of contingencies which were bound to arise. In this case, planning and experience did make a difference.

A campaign of this nature inevitably had its heroes; surprisingly it exhibited few leaders who were either negligent or incompetent. The German generals at Marseilles and Toulon, Schaefer and Bässler, might have made a more determined effort to hold out longer, but the overall commander, General Blaskowitz, certainly directed his forces in retreat with great skill and imagination. The Allied generals also performed well. While General Dahlquist was not as aggressive as some in his initial combat experience, General Patch and especially General Truscott showed themselves to be dynamic, aggressive leaders. (It is regrettable that Patch died soon after the war of pneumonia.) The same dynamism applied to General de Lattre, the French commander, who was instrumental in molding the French units into a vigorous fighting force. Jacob Devers's role was somewhat different, but his continuing advocacy of a southern France operation was important in assuring that the American viewpoint prevailed.

Among the naval and air commanders, General Eaker, head of the Mediterranean Allied Air Forces, General Saville at the tactical air level, and Admiral Hewitt stand out. The latter, a veteran of numerous amphibious campaigns, was especially effective in seeing that the invasion phase of Dragoon was carried through on time and in a relatively smooth manner.

A number of combat units also distinguished themselves. Most outstanding were the Allied lead divisions, the United States 3rd, 45th, and 36th. Each of them scored noteworthy triumphs—the 3rd during the initial stages of the invasion, the 36th north of Montélimar, the 45th in the race for the Belfort Gap. Not only did these three divisions see heavy fighting during Dragoon, but after the war it was found that they had suffered the heaviest casualties of all the American divisions which had served during World War II.[2] Of the French formations, General Monsabert's 3rd Algerian Division was particularly effective, especially in its exploits at Toulon and Marseilles. While one can overromanticize the role of the various Resistance groups, they no doubt helped ease the intelligence and combat burdens of the regular forces. On the German side, the 11th Panzer Division's skillful rearguard action prevented Allied units from capturing the bulk of the Axis forces as they hastily withdrew northward.

Nevertheless, tactically, it is difficult to fault the Allied field commanders. On the whole, they showed an aggressive spirit and attempted with the help of timely intelligence to exploit their advantages—in the face of enemy weakness—to the fullest extent. To be sure, in the battle for the Montélimar quadrilateral and again in the push toward Belfort, they were too tentative and failed to cut off the retreating German forces.[3] But a 400-mile advance, the capture of Toulon and Marseilles, and a junction with Eisenhower's forces within a month represent considerable achievements and cannot be argued away.[4]

To say that Dragoon was an outstanding tactical success,

however, still begs the essential strategic question: Was the French Riviera campaign truly necessary? After the war, the debate between the Americans and the British regarding the Provençal invasion continued, though in muted form. Not surprisingly, most American leaders persisted in their belief that the operation was both necessary and beneficial to the Allied cause. To General Marshall, who was not given to overstatement, "The southern France operation was one of the most successful things we did."[5] General Eisenhower echoed Marshall's sentiments when he wrote that "there was no development of that period which added more decisively to our advantage or aided us more in accomplishing the final and complete defeat of the German forces than did this secondary attack coming up the Rhone Valley." To General Devers, "The operation on the southern coast of France will go down as a classic for . . . exploitation, and results."

As is often the case when questions become historical, in more recent years the American position has begun to shift. In particular, historians Coakley and Leighton in 1969 wrote that Dragoon contributed nothing to Overlord logistically and that it was probably decisive only in prolonging the campaign in Italy.[6]

Their view obviously corresponds closely with what the British themselves were writing soon after the war. Churchill, of course, had little good to say about Dragoon in his memoirs. "When it was belatedly launched," he points out, "it drew no enemy down from the Normandy battle theatre," and "therefore none of the reasons present in our minds at Teheran had any relation to what was done and Dragoon caused no diversion from the forces opposing General Eisenhower."[7] Churchill goes on to say, "In fact instead of helping Eisenhower, he helped it by threatening the rear of the Germans retiring up the Rhone Valley." The wartime Prime Minister does admit "that the operation as carried out eventually brought important assistance to General Eisenhower by the arrival of another army on his right flank," and that it did open up another line of communications. But he still concludes that the price was not worth the effort, for "the army of Italy was deprived of its opportunity to strike a most formidable blow at the Germans, and very possibly to reach Vienna, with all that might have followed therefrom." Chester Wilmot, the Australian historian killed in 1954, was equally adamant in his condemnation of Dragoon, though from a slightly different perspective.

The decision to switch the Mediterranean *Schwerpunkt* from Italy to southern France meant that from the start of July until the middle of August . . . the Allied assault along the whole southern flank of Europe was deliberately weakened and drastically curtailed. . . . Having distorted Allied strategy in the Mediterranean, Operation Anvil was now to contribute to the distortion of Allied strategy in the West; to the immediate benefit of Hitler and the ultimate advantage of Stalin.[8]

But like the American position, that of British writers has also moved away from outright condemnation of the French Riviera campaign. In 1960, Lord Ismay, the secretary to the British Chiefs of Staff and also to Churchill, while tying in the Dragoon decision with Soviet control of eastern Europe, asserts that "from the military point of view, Dragoon was fully justified," and that the introduction of French units onto their own soil was a positive result of the operation.[9] And in the same year the noted naval historian, Capt. S. W. (now Sir Stephen) Roskill, though tending to favor the Italian alternative, refrains from drawing definite conclusions about whether or not the carrying out of Dragoon was justified.

While the above "after the fact" debate raises a number of interesting issues, it does little to solve the problem at hand. A better approach from an historical standpoint is to ask if Dragoon actually accomplished what it was intended to accomplish at the time. Did it, as originally envisaged, contain substantial numbers of Wehrmacht troops in southern France? Did it make the most effective use of French forces? Did the liberation of the main ports in the area make a difference in the ability of the Allies to replenish and expand their forces? And within a broader context, to what extent did Dragoon alter Anglo-American strategy?

The first question is exceedingly difficult to answer, for the answer depends to a large extent on the period one is discussing. If we ask, did the French Riviera campaign support Overlord by forcing Germany to retain her forces in southern France, the answer has to be no. In fact, it had just the opposite effect. Since Dragoon (or Anvil at the time) was not launched simultaneously with Overlord, the Germans were able to move substantial numbers of soldiers (including entire divisions) and equipment from the south to assist in the Normandy battle.

But if we consider the question from the standpoint that Dragoon did not take place at the same time as Overlord, but ten weeks after it (as actually happened), then the answer is quite different. No matter how depleted the Axis forces were, the Germans still had to keep considerable numbers of formations positioned along France's Mediterranean coast. In this sense, particularly after August 7, when the Germans knew that the Allies were definitely building up their forces for an attack, Dragoon did restrain the Wehrmacht from sending additional men and material north. This a threat alone would not have accomplished.

In a more direct sense, the French Riviera campaign also fulfilled its original purpose by netting the Allies 79,000 prisoners, losses which were becoming increasingly impossible for the Wehrmacht to replace. And this number would have been even greater had it not been for the determined German effort to assure that the bulk of its troops were able to elude the various traps set by the Allies. On the other hand, one might contend that Germany's rapid withdrawal from the south was a blessing in disguise, for it forced Germany to consolidate her forces in eastern France and to establish a much more formidable defensive barrier than if there had been no retreat. What all of this reasoning indicates, of course, is that there is a certain ambivalence as to whether Dragoon fulfilled its original purpose of drawing off large numbers of German troops.

The second question can be answered with more assurance. The Riviera operation obviously did make the most effective use of French forces at the time. While having fought well in Italy, French leaders wanted their units engaged in combat on French soil and pressed the Americans and British at every opportunity to make sure that their desire became a reality. The argument that French troops could have been introduced more quickly through Bordeaux or Brittany or even Antwerp is based on a misperception of the situation. The French military effort was centered in the Mediterranean, and it would have been virtually impossible to mount an offensive from there against the Bay of Biscay coast. Moreover, as of August 15, Bordeaux, the Breton ports, and Antwerp were still in German hands, and the harbors being used for Overlord were already stretched to the limit. They could not have handled additional French troops, even if the latter could have been moved to England. Finally, once the invasion of southern France had taken place, French forces benefited from having their ranks swelled by large numbers of local recruits. The American official historian estimates that the French contribution saved the United

States alone from having to send eight to ten divisions into combat into Europe.[10] These soldiers could be put to good use in the Pacific and elsewhere.

Regarding the use of French Mediterranean ports, there is little doubt that they fulfilled and possibly even exceeded the Allies' expectations. Their early capture had taken on added urgency when General Marshall contended (truthfully) in June that he had thirty to forty divisions in the United States that could be shipped to Europe and that they could be utilized most expeditiously by being introduced through Toulon and Marseilles.[11] But the German surrender at the end of August still did not provide the Allies with sufficient port and rail capacity to have a decisive effect in 1944.

What Toulon and Marseilles did do was to clear almost immediately the western Mediterranean of enemy ships and aircraft.[12] More importantly, their capture allowed Eisenhower to carry through his "broad front" strategy in 1945.[13] Between September 1944 and the end of the war, the Allies unloaded 4,123,725 long tons of cargo and 915,515 troops (mostly through Marseilles) into southern France. On a monthly basis one-third to one-fourth of the goods supplied to the European theater came through these ports (including Port-du-Bouc for gasoline). To be sure, they never possessed the capacity to supply much more than Devers's southern group of armies on the western front, but his Sixth Army Group assuredly benefited a good deal during the spring of 1945 from its supply links to Toulon and Marseilles, links which would have been more difficult to forge elsewhere.

This large influx of men and supplies relates directly to our last question: To what extent did Dragoon alter Allied strategy? Obviously it played an important role in committing the British and the Americans unalterably to a western strategy. It was not a minor diversion. A three-divisional assault, backed up by a large naval and air armada, was a sizable undertaking even (one might say especially) at this stage of the war. And the American and French commitment to the area—first as a combat front, and later as a supply conduit—is ample evidence that southern France should not be perceived as one of the war's forgotten theaters.

A different appraisal of this question has been offered by historian Charles MacDonald. His view is that "given the scope of Allied victory in Normandy, the Germans probably would have withdrawn from southern France without a second invasion."[14] But his assertion is difficult to uphold. While German military leaders at the highest level considered this possibility, and those in the field urged it, there is no evidence that they would have taken this step even after American forces had broken out in the north and were advancing at a rapid rate. In fact, one might ask what the Allies would have done to protect their southern flank as it extended across France? Might not the Germans, especially their mobile and armored formations south of the Loire, have posed a threat to Patton's Third Army in spite of aerial superiority as well as the other way around?

A more potent argument is that the troops used in Dragoon could have been better employed in Italy. This was Churchill's position all along, and there is some justification for it. The problem with this kind of thinking is that strengthening the forces in Italy did not guarantee the collapse of Germany, and any Allied attempt to push past northern Italy and through the Ljubljana Gap would have been exceedingly difficult to carry through and to support logistically.

Churchill's view (shared by others) has also been linked with his desire to forestall Soviet control over eastern Europe, a desire thwarted by the United States's supposed naïveté regarding the political realities in Europe. But Churchill's motives at this juncture seem to have been different.[15] While obviously perturbed about the Soviet threat, he was more concerned about strengthening the British-dominated front in Italy than he was in meeting the threat by undertaking a full-scale operation in the Balkans. That he advocated a more openly aggressive policy toward the Soviets later on should not be read into the situation in August and September 1944.

And this leads to the final point. Whatever Churchill or his Chiefs of Staff considered the correct strategy, the Americans were determined to have a campaign in southern France, and by this time in the war they almost always got their way. In fact, after the Washington Conference in May 1943 it is difficult to find an instance when the United States did not dictate Anglo-American strategy. Whether it was America's Pacific strategy, her emphasis on northern Burma (to supply more adequately Chiang Kai-shek), her advocacy of Overlord, or her later "broad front" strategy, the British really had little alternative but to go along with American thinking. The Americans had obviously become the dominant partner in the western alliance. In this respect, the necessity of the French Riviera campaign actually becomes a moot point. Unless the United States changed its mind, sooner or later Dragoon was bound to be executed.

In summary, then, after a year-long debate between British and American leaders, the French Riviera operation was finally launched. Its tactical success has not, however, led to its strategic acceptance. Long after Dragoon was over, the British in particular have continued to question its necessity. Their most telling point is that by undertaking the Provençal invasion, the Italian campaign was weakened beyond repair, and this eventually confined the United States and British solely to a western strategy in late 1944 and 1945. But the Americans still insist that their strategy was the correct one. In their view, the operation in southern France kept Hitler's forces reeling, it heightened France's contribution to the war effort, and it opened up additional ports which helped the Allies sustain their offensives in 1945. The important point is that while Dragoon may not have been decisive in winning the war, it was a highly significant operation, and it reflects the United States's decisive influence in the Anglo-American partnership.

Appendix

Notes

Bibliography

Index

Appendix

CODE NAMES

ALPHA: Landing beaches used by the United States 3rd Division in the Dragoon invasion.

ANTON: Axis occupation of France's Vichy zone, November 11–12, 1942.

ANVIL: Allied plan for the invasion of southern France; eventually launched as Operation Dragoon.

AXIS: German takeover of areas occupied by Italian forces, September 9–11, 1943.

BUCCANEER: Allied plan for an amphibious operation against the Andaman and Nicobar Islands, west of Burma.

CAIMAN: De Gaulle's plan to airlift French paratroopers into central France, July 1944.

CAMEL: Landing beaches used by United States 36th Division in the French Riviera campaign.

DELTA: Landing beaches used by United States 45th Division in the Dragoon operation.

DRAGOON: Successor to Anvil, the Allied plan for the invasion of southern France; launched on August 15, 1944.

DUCROT: Allied air operations after the initial Dragoon landings.

FERDINAND: Allied deception measures carried out in conjunction with Operation Dragoon.

LILA: Takeover of Toulon and its environs by German 7th Panzer Division, November 27, 1942.

NUTMEG: Allied air operation prior to Dragoon, from D − 5 to 3:50 A.M. on D day.

OVERLORD: Overall Allied plan and operation for the invasion of Normandy, June 6, 1944.

ROMEO: French commandos who attacked the French coast west of the main Dragoon invasion force.

ROSIE: French marines who landed east of the main Dragoon invasion force.

RUGBY: Allied airborne troops who were dropped behind the Provençal coast in conjunction with Operation Dragoon.

SITKA: Allied commandos who assaulted the offshore islands of Port-Cros and Levant, August 15, 1944.

YOKUM: Allied air operations immediately prior to Dragoon, from 3:50 to 7:30 A.M., August 15, 1944.

Notes

CHAPTER 1. THE ANVIL DEBATE

1. CCS 303/2, "Strategic Concept for the Defeat of the Axis in Europe," 16 Aug. 1943, CAB 88/15, PRO.

2. AFHQ, A93528, "Operations to Assist Overlord," 27 Oct. 1943, RG 218, CCS 381, France (7–28–43), NA.

3. JP(43) 391(Final), "Operation 'Anvil,'" 5 Nov. 1943, CAB 79/67, PRO.

4. COS(43) 791 (o), Part 2, 25 Feb. 1944, CAB 80/77, PRO.

5. Ehrman, *Grand Strategy*, 5:176–77.

6. AFHQ, P-122, "Anvil: Appreciation and Outline Plan," 22 Dec. 1943, RG 218, CCS 381, France (7–28–43), Sec. 2, Pt. 1, NA.

7. Marshall to Devers, 28 Dec. 1943, Devers Papers, Sec. 18, Folder 16, York, Pa.

8. Eaker to Harris, 4 Feb. 1944, Eaker Papers, Box 7, File 11, LC.

9. As cited in Pogue, *George C. Marshall*, 374.

10. CCS 446/1, "Three-Division Lift for 'Anvil,'" 8 Jan. 1944, CAB 88/21, PRO.

11. Matloff, *Strategic Planning*, 374.

12. CCS 465/3, "Recommendations . . . ," 31 Jan. 1944, CAB 88/23, PRO. Italics mine.

13. CCS 465/4, "Recommendations . . . ," 4 Feb. 1944, CAB 88/23, PRO.

14. Griess/Eaker Interview, 1973, Devers Papers, Tape 58, York, Pa.

15. Dill to Chiefs of Staff, 5 Feb. 1944, PREM 3/342, PRO.

16. Matloff, *Strategic Planning*, 420–21; Special Meeting, "Meeting between President and Joint Chiefs of Staff," 21 Feb. 1944, RG 218, CCS 334, NA; and CCS 465/10, "Recommendations . . . ," 24 Feb. 1944, CAB 88/23, PRO.

17. COS(44) 278(0), "Operation 'Anvil,'" 21 Mar. 1944, CAB 80/81. PRO.

18. Seventh Army, "Diary," Jan. 27–Feb. 24, 1944, CMH; and Hewitt, "Invasion of Southern France, Report of Naval Commander, Western Task Force," 15 Nov. 1944, 1, NHD.

19. Eaker to Brownell, 21 19 Feb. 1944, Eaker Papers, Box 7, File 11, LC.

20. Ibid.

21. Letter, Forrest C. Pogue to author, 19 Jan. 1979.

22. Griess/Devers Interview, 1969, Devers Papers, Tape 24, York, Pa.

23. Hewitt, Transcript of Oral History, Reel 24/44, NHD.

24. Headquarters Force 163, X-440, "Tentative Army Outline Plan, Operation 'Anvil,'" 29 Mar. 1944, RG 338, Hq. 7th Army, G-3, Plans and Operations 1943–44, General Archives Division, WNRC.

CHAPTER 2. GERMAN STRATEGY AND DEFENSES

1. AOK 1, 187/43 g.Kdos.Ch., "Befehl," 7.11.42, T312/24/7530254, NA.

2. AOK 1, "Kriegstagebuch," 10.11.42, T-312/24/7530871, NA.

3. Schramm et al., KTB/OKW 288

4. Auphan and Mordal, *The French Navy in World War II*, 258–59.

5. Ibid., 261; and 7. Pz. Division, 26.11.42, T-315/426/000377, NA.

6. Armeegruppe Felber, Ia 425/43 g.K., "Bericht . . . ," 21,7, 43, T-312/978/9170130–205, NA.

7. Armeegruppe Felber, Ia 1750/43 g.Kdos., T-312/978/ 9170216, 9170234–43, NA.

8. AOK 19, "Kriegstagebuch," 31.7.43, T-312/977/9167823, NA.

9. Obkdo. von Sodenstern, 394/43 g.Kdos.Chefs., 20.8.43, T-312/977/9168361, NA.

10. AOK 19, 31.8.43, T-312/977/9168534, NA.

11. AOK 19, "Kriegstagebuch," 8.9.43, T-312/977/9167928, NA.

12. AOK 19, 6063/43 g.Kdos., 9.9.43, T-312/978/9169168, NA.

13. AOK 19, "Tatigkeitsbericht . . . ," n.d., T-312/978/ 9170877–78, NA.

14. Oberbefehsshaber West, 550/43 g.K.Ch., 28.10.43, T-311/ 277/032424–74, NA.

15. As translated in Harrison, *Cross-Channel Attack*, 464. The original German version is published in Hubatsch, ed., *Hitlers Weisungen für die Kriegführung*, 233.

16. Vogel, FMS, B575/39–46, NA; and Krueger, FMS, B486/ 11–13, NA.

17. Zimmermann, FMS, B308/60, NA.

18. Ob West, 1904/42 g.Kdos., 16. Dez. 1944, T-78/317/ 6271545–46, NA; and Vogel, FMS, B575/41–42, NA.

19. Ob West, Ia 1173/44 geh.Kdos., 7.2.44, T-311/247/026073; Ob West, Ia 4366/44 geh.Kdos., 5.6.44, T-311/247/029526.

20. Der Oberbefehlshaber der Armeegruppe G, Ia 1598/44 g.Kdos., "Lage bei 19. Armee," T-311/140/7185841, NA.

21. Kontrollinspektion der DWSTK, 890/44 geh., "Monatsbericht," 7 Juli 1944, T-77/848/5592321, NA; and AGr G, 7.7.44, T-311/140/7185089, NA.

22. Oberkommando AGr G, 1459/44 g.Kdos., 28.7.1944, T-311/140/7189699, NA; and Obkdo. Armeegruppe G, Ia 1364 g.Kdos., "Tagesmeldung," 24.7.1944, T-311/140/7185665.

23. Foot, *SOE in France*, 393. A full-length version of the Vercors tragedy is available in Pearson, *Tears of Glory.*

24. Buechs, FMS, A869/1–3, NA; and Hewitt, "Invasion of Southern France," 45–46, NHD. Hewitt's Eighth Fleet estimate, when compared against the less complete Foreign Military Studies, seems quite accurate.

25. Armeegruppe G, 2.8.44, T-311/140/185153.

CHAPTER 3. ANVIL BECOMES DRAGOON

1. Lincoln to Roberts, 22 Mar. 1944, RG 319, ABC File 384, NA.

2. CCS 465/13, "'Overlord' and 'Anvil,'" 24 Mar. 1944, CAB 88/23, PRO.

3. CCS 465/14, "'Overlord' and 'Anvil,'" 28 Mar. 1944, CAB 88/23, PRO.

4. CCS, 154th Meeting, 8 Apr. 1944, CAB 88/4, PRO.

5. Matloff, *Strategic Planning*, 426.

6. Bryant, *Triumph in the West*, 148.

7. CCS, 158th Meeting, 28 Apr. 1944, CAB 88/4, PRO.

8. Wilson to Chiefs of Staff, 17 May 1944, WO 204/1634, PRO.

9. Vigneras, *Rearming the French*, 178; and de Lattre, *History of the First French Army*, 29.

10. De Lattre, *History of the First French Army*, 11–12.

11. Truscott, *Command Missions*, 386.

12. Vigneras, *Rearming the French*, 169.

13. *New York Times*, 6 June 1944, 1.

14. SHAEF, G-3, "Planners' View on Use of Mediterranean Reserve," 11 June 1944, RG 331, SHAEF File, NA; and CCS 163d Meeting, 11 June 1944, CAB 88/4, PRO.

15. Pogue, *George C. Marshall*, 406.

16. SHAEF, S54425, 23 June 1944, RG 218, Leahy File, 16, NA.

17. COS(44), 206th Meeting(O), 22 June 1944, CAB 99/76, PRO.

18. CCS 603/1, "Operations to Assist Overlord," 27 June 1944, CAB 88/28, PRO.

19. CCS 603/2, "Operations to Assist Overlord," 27 June 1944, CAB 88/28, PRO.

20. SHAEF, 27 June 1944, WO 204/1634, PRO.

21. Eisenhower to Marshall, S54760, 29 June 1944, RG 218, Leahy File, 16, NA.

22. COS(44)585, "Operations in the European Theater," 29 June 1944, CAB 80/85, PRO.

23. Ehrman, *Grand Strategy*, 5:355–57.

24. Marshall to Eisenhower, 8 July 1944, WO 204/1635, PRO.

25. Eaker to Arnold, 16 July 1944, Eaker Papers, Box 22, LC.

26. Churchill, *Triumph and Tragedy*, 589.

27. CCS 603/15, "Operations to Assist Overlord," 5 Aug. 1944, CAB 88/28, PRO.

28. Churchill, *Triumph and Tragedy*, 57–60.

29. Headquarters, Seventh Army, X-1317, "Field Order #1 (Anvil)," 29 July 1944, RG 407, File 107-3.9, General Archives Division, WNRC; and COS(44) 713(o), "Operation Dragoon," 9 Aug. 1944, CAB 80/86, PRO.

30. Truscott, *Command Missions*, 383.

31. Dahlquist to wife, Ruth, 10 July 1944, Dahlquist Papers, USAMHRC.

32. De Lattre, *History of the First French Army*, 54.

33. COS(44) 712(o), "Operation Dragoon," 9 Aug. 1944, CAB 80/86, PRO; and Roskill, *The War at Sea*, 3, pt. 2, 91.

34. Seventh Army, File A4-3–95, "Operations Plan 4-44," 29 July 1944, RG 407, File 107-3.5, General Archives Division, WNRC; and Headquarters, Twelfth Air Force, "XII Air Force Service Command in Operation Dragoon," n.d., 1–2, USAMHRC.

35. Craven and Cate, eds., *Europe: Argument to V-E Day*, 420–25; Commander US Naval Forces, Northwest African Waters, "Naval Forces, Northwest African Waters and the Eighth Fleet,"

1945, 41–44, NHD; and XL5945, 130557Z/8/44, DEFE 3/117, PRO.

36. As cited in Craven and Cate, eds., *Europe: Argument to V-E Day*, 415.

37. Office of Strategic Services, *War Report*, 2:233–38, NA; and AFHQ, G-3, SI OPS Section, "History of Special Operations, Mediterranean Theater, 1942–1945," 24 July 1945, RG 407, File 95-AL1-3.0, General Archives Division, WNRC.

38. Armeegruppe G, "Lagebeurteilung," 7.8.44, T-311/140/7185871; Armeegruppe G, 12.8.44, T-311/140/7185931, NA; and XL6079, 130204 5Z/8/44, DEFE 3/118, PRO.

39. As cited in Guiral, *Libération de Marseille*, 28.

40. *New York Times*, 12 Aug. 1944, 1,4.

41. Obkdo. AGr G, Ia 1741/44 g.Kdos., 10.8.44, T-311/140/7185903, NA.

42. Wilutzky, FMS A882/1–5, NA; Guiral, *Libération de Marseille*, 81; and Morison, *The Invasion of France and Germany*, 239–40.

43. Von Wietersheim, FMS A880/1–2; and Drews FMS A881/1–3, NA.

44. XL5071, 071008Z/8/44, DEFE 3/114, PRO; and Ruhfus, FMS B556/18, NA.

45. Buechs, FMS A869/2–3, NA.

46. Kahn, "The Ultra Conference."

CHAPTER 4. THE INVASION

1. Hewitt, "Invasion of Southern France," 37–41, NHD; Roskill, *War at Sea*, 3, pt. 2, 92; and US Army, "Invasion of Southern France," 31, CMH.

2. Truscott, *Command Missions*, 409.

3. *Life Magazine*, 2 Oct. 1944, 97.

4. Dahlquist to wife, Ruth, 14 Aug. 1944, Dahlquist Papers, USAMHRC.

5. 3ID(Reinf), "Field Order No. 12," 1 Aug. 1944, 3rd Infantry Division Collection, USAMHRC; Taggart, ed., *History of the Third Infantry Division in World War II*, 199–202.

6. Nelson, *Thunderbird: A History of the 45th Infantry Division*, 72.

7. *A Pictorial History of the 36th "Texas" Infantry Division*, passim.

8. Wietersheim, FMS, A880/3, NA.

9. The combat portion of the narrative which follows is based primarily on US Army, "Invasion of Southern France," passim, CMH.

10. Ibid., 44; Craven and Cate, eds., *Europe: Argument to V-E Day*, 427–428; AG 370.2/171 GCT-0, "Report on Airborne Operations in Dragoon," 25 Oct. 1944, WO 204/1625, PRO; SHAEF, "Report on Airborne Operations and Seaborne Operations in the Initial Stages of Operation DRAGOON," RG 331, SHAEF File, G-3, NA; and "Report on Airborne Operations in Dragoon," Eaker Papers, Box 24, LC. For an overview, see Huston, *Out of the Blue: U.S. Army Airborne Operations in World War II*.

11. *New York Times*, 16 Aug. 1944, 4.

12. Hewitt, "Invasion of Southern France," 45–47, NHD; [Seventh Army], File No. A-16.3, 1 Oct. 1944, RG 407, File 107-3.0, General Archives Division, WNRC; and Roskill, *War at Sea*, 3, pt. 2. 96.

13. Hewitt, "Invasion of Southern France," 45, NHD; Craven and Cate, eds., *Europe: Argument to V-E Day*, 428; Morison, *The Invasion of France and Germany*, 251, 256–57; de Lattre, *History of the First French Army*, 66; and US Army, "Invasion of Southern France," 46–51, CMH.

14. *New York Times*, 15 Aug. 1944, 1.

15. Our discussion of the assault phase and its aftermath is taken mainly from US Army, "Invasion of Southern France," passim, CMH; and Morison, *The Invasion of France and Germany*, passim. The published Seventh Army history follows the theater history closely, but lacks its authoritativeness.

16. US Army, "Invasion of Southern France," 64–69, CMH.

17. Ibid., 53–54.

18. Morison, *The Invasion of France and Germany*, 271–72.

19. Truscott, *Command Missions*, 414.

20. Palmer/Devers Interview, 1969, Devers Papers, Tape 2, York, Pa.

21. US Army, "Invasion of Southern France," 252–53, CMH.

22. Staiger, *Rückzug durchs Rhônetal*, 41–42; Baptist Kniess, FMS, B376/3–4, NA; Hewitt, "Invasion of Southern France," 46, NHD; XL6464, 160025Z/8/44, DEFE 3/119, PRO; and XL6810, 180140Z/8/44, DEFE 3/121, PRO.

23. Ibid., 53; Craven and Cates, eds., *Europe: Argument to V-E Day*, 429–30; US Army, "Invasion of Southern France," 52, CMH; US Seventh Army, CPX 12475, 17 Aug. 1944, Message File, Dragoon 1, NHD; Roskill, *War at Sea*, 3, pt. 2, 99; [Seventh Army], File No. A4-3/N95, "Operations Plan 4-44," 29 July 1944, RG 407, File 107-3.5, General Archives Division, WNRC; and Office of Rear Admiral, Escort Carriers, No. 414/E.C. ADM 199/910, PRO; and letter, Dean C. Allard to author, 1 Nov. 1979.

24. Dahlquist to wife, Ruth, 17 Aug. [1944], Dahlquist Papers, USAMHRC.

25. *New York Times*, 15 Aug. 1944, 18.

26. SHAEF Log, "Dragoon Diary," RG 331, SHAEF File, G-3, NA; and US Army, "Invasion of Southern France," passim, CMH.

27. US Army, "Invasion of Southern France," 102–3, CMH.

28. Hewitt, "Invasion of Southern France," 55–56, NHD; MAAF, MX 28401, 17 Aug. 1944, Message File, Dragoon 1, NHD; and Craven and Cate, eds., *Europe: Argument to V-E Day*, 431.

29. De Lattre, *History of the First French Army*, 68.

30. Ibid., 64; AFHQ, "History of Special Operations," RG 407, File 95AL1-3.0, General Archives Division, WNRC; and Office of Strategic Services *War Report*, 2:241–42, NA.

31. US Army, "Invasion of Southern France," 136–37, CMH.

32. Ibid., 107–8.

33. De Lattre, *History of the First French Army*, 71–75; and Truscott, *Command Missions*, 421–22.

34. CG, AFHQ, BX 15785, 19 Aug. 1944, Message File, Dragoon 1, NHD; Hewitt, "Invasion of Southern France," 58–65, NHD; Craven and Cate, eds., *Europe: Argument to V-E Day*, 433–36; and Headquarters, 64th Fighter Wing, "XII Tactical Air Command: Tactical Operations," 18 Apr. 1945, 66–67, USAMHRC.

35. Armeegruppe G, Ia Nr. 1926/44 g.Kdos., 17.8.44, T-311/140/7185993, NA; Armeegruppe G, Ia Nr. 1933/44 g.Kdos.Ch., 18.8.44, T-311/140/7185401–2; and Schaefer, FMS, A884/8–10.

36. Forty Panther tanks were still west of the river, however. (XL6491, 221814Z/8/44, DEFE 3/123, PRO.)

37. XL7471, 221546Z/8/44, DEFE 3/123, PRO; XL7435, 220348Z/8/44, DEFE 3/123, PRO; and Morison, *The Invasion of France and Germany*, 257.

38. US Army, "Invasion of Southern France," 180–81, CMH; Eaker to Arnold, 21 Aug. 1944, Eaker Papers, Box 22, LC; Cunningham Correspondence, Vol. XXI, Add MS 52577, British Museum Library; and XL6919, 181356Z/8/44, DEFE 3/121, PRO.

39. Seventh Army, "Diary," Aug. 18 and 19, CMH; Adjutant General's Section, Ref. No.C-2518, 18 Aug 44, RG 331, Hq. VI Army Gp, File 1944, No. 7, NA; and Eaker to Arnold, 21 Aug. 1944, Eaker Papers, Box 22, LC.

40. Lt. Comdr. J. Staniforth, "South of France, Operation 'Dragoon,' 'Alpha Red' Sector," 14 Sept. 1944, ADM 199/910, PRO; US Army, "Invasion of Southern France," 137–38, CMH; and Seventh Army, "Diary," 20 Aug. 1944, CMH.

41. Hewitt, "Invasion of Southern France," 68, NHD; and AFHQ Advance, BX 15806, 21 Aug. 1944, Message File, Dragoon 1, NHD.

42. Eisenhower to AFHQ for Wilson, 24 Aug. 1944, Chandler, ed., *The Papers of Dwight David Eisenhower*, 4:2095.

CHAPTER 5. THE CHASE

1. Headquarters, Seventh Army, "Field Order #2(Dragoon),"19 Aug. 1944, RG 407, File no. 107-3.9, General Archives Division, WNRC.

2. The Toulon and Marseilles operations are based on US Army, "Invasion of Southern France," passim, CMH, and de Lattre, *History of the French First Army*, passim.

3. KTB/OKW, 4:266, 277–78.

4. US Eighth Fleet to Seventh Army, "The Effects of Aerial Bombardment and Naval Gunfire on the Defenses of Saint Mandrier," 4 Oct. 1944, RG 407, File 107-0.10, General Archives Division, WNRC; and Morison, *The Invasion of France and Germany*, 287–88.

5. De Lattre, *History of the French First Army*, 73.

6. US Army, "Invasion of Southern France," 151, CMH.

7. Ibid., 159–60.

8. De Lattre, *History of the French First Army*, 94.

9. Ibid., 108.

10. Schaefer, FMS, A884/34, NA.

11. Seventh Army, "Diary," passim, and US Army, "Invasion of Southern France," passim, CMH.

12. US Army, "Invasion of Southern France," 200, CMH.

13. Ibid., 251–52. Ultra information about Grenoble is revealed in XL7493, 221849Z/8/44, DEFE 3/123, PRO.

14. US Army, "Invasion of Southern France," Appendices A and B, CMH; and Staiger, *Rückzug durchs Rhônetal*, passim.

15. Truscott, *Command Missions*, 427. Truscott's key role is clarified in a letter from Gen. Theodore J. Conway to the author, 1 Nov. 1979.

16. The exchange between Truscott and Dahlquist is covered in US Army, "Invasion of Southern France," 235–36, CMH.

17. Wietersheim, FMS, A880/7–12, NA; Drews, FMS, A881/3;

Baptist Kniess, FMS, A888/7–8, NA; and XL 7830, 250828Z/8/44, DEFE 3/125, PRO.

18. Truscott, *Command Missions*, 430–31.

19. Dahlquist to wife, Ruth, 29 Aug. 1944, Dahlquist Papers, USAMHRC.

20. Truscott, *Command Missions*, 433.

21. Seiz, FMS, A960/1–3, NA.

22. Fretter-Pico, FMS, B203/4–6. For an exciting account of the Resistance's role, see Leslie, *The Liberation of the Riviera.*

23. US Army, "Invasion of Southern France," 234, CMH.

24. Seventh Army, *Report of Operations*, 1:244–46.

25. Ibid., 223–26.

26. Hewitt, "Invasion of Southern France," 86–98, CMH.

27. Ibid., 94; AFHQ to War Office, 28 Aug. 1944, WO 106/4008, PRO; AFHQ to Seventh Army, FX 90557, 1 Sep 1944, RG 331, VI Army Group, File no. 383-6, NA; and Wilson to British Chiefs of Staff, 2 Sept. 1944, WO 106/4008, PRO.

28. Devers to Maj. Gen. L. W. Rooks, 22 Aug. 1944, and Devers to Rooks, 23 Aug. 1944, Devers Papers, Sec. 19, Folder 21, York, Pa; and CCS to Wilson, Octagon 23, 13 Sept. 1944, RG 331, VI Army Group, File 381-1, NA.

29. De Lattre, *History of the French First Army*, 134; and Headquarters, Seventh Army, "Field Order #4," 28 Aug. 1944, RG 407, File 107-3.9, General Archives Division, WNRC.

30. Headquarters, VI Corps, "Planning Estimate and Recommendations," Theodore J. Conway Papers, USAMHRC; Seventh Army, "Diary," passim, CMH and *The Fighting 36th*, passim.

31. Dahlquist to wife, Ruth, 20 Aug. 1944, Dahlquist Papers, USAMHRC.

32. Staiger, *Rückzug durchs Rhônetal*, 97; and Wilutzky, FMS, A882/24.

33. De Lattre, *History of the French First Army*, 126.

34. Truscott, *Command Missions*, 439.

35. Seventh Army, *Report of Operations*, 1: 223–25.

36. Griess/Devers Interview, 1969, Devers Papers, Tape 24, York, Pa.

37. Seventh Army, "Diary," 2 and 3 Sept. 1944; AFHQ to British Chiefs of Staff, FX 91460, 4 Sept. 1944, RG 331, SHAEF File, Dragoon 370.37, NA; XL8240, 280219Z/8/44, DEFE 3/126, PRO; and XL7915, 252135Z/8/44, DEFE 3/125, PRO.

38. De Lattre, *History of the French First Army*, 132.

39. Taggart, ed., *History of the Third Infantry Division*, 224–29; and Seventh Army, *Report of Operations*, 1: 262.

40. Seventh Army, *Report of Operations*, 1: 271–72; and Maigne, "Les Forces françaises et la jonction 'Overlord-Dragoon,'" 17.

41. Nelson, *Thunderbird: A History of the 45th Infantry Division*, 77.

42. Botsch, FMS, B518/26, NA.

43. Eaker to Cannon, 9 Sept. 1944, Eaker Papers, Box 23, LC.

44. von Gyldenfeldt, FMS, B558/14–16, NA.

45. Headquarters, Seventh Army, "Field Order #5," 14 Sept. 1944, RG 407, File 107-3.9, General Archives Division, WNRC; and Truscott, *Command Missions*, 441–44.

46. Palmer/Devers Interview, 1969, Devers Papers, Tape 3, York, Pa.; and Griess/Jenkins Interview, 1970, Devers Papers, Tape 34, York, Pa.

47. Dahlquist to wife, Ruth, 5 Sept. 1944, Dahlquist Papers, USAMHRC.

48. AFHQ to Seventh Army, FX 23679, 11 Sept. 1944, RG 331, VI Army Group, File 360.42, NA; and Arnold to Eisenhower, FX 29133, 12 Sept. 1944, RG 331, VI Army Group, File 360.42, NA.

49. Dahlquist to Brig. Gen. Ed O. Betts, 21 Nov. 1944, Dahlquist Papers, USAMHRC; Marcel Billon to Monsieur l'Ambassador, 22 Sept. 1944, RG 331, VI Army Group, File 250.1, NA; and "Sandy" Patch to Eaker, 2 Sept. 1944, Eaker Papers, Box 25, File 17, LC.

50. Hewitt, "Invasion of Southern France," 15 Sept. 1944, 117,

and 25 Sept. 1944, 133; Devers, "Operation Dragoon," 41; and *History of MAAF*, April 1945, 137, Eaker Papers, Box 27, LC.

CHAPTER 6. AN ASSESSMENT

1. Office of the Commander-in-Chief, Mediterranean, Allied Forces Headquarters, "Dragoon," 2nd June 1945, ADM 199/909, PRO.

2. *New York Times*, April 14, 1946, 2.

3. De Lattre, for instance, wrote: "The 7th Army's chief had not seemed as determined as General Truscott to continue the pursuit in the Belfort direction whatever the cost" (*History of the First French Army*, 143).

4. Supreme Allied Commander [Wilson], "Invasion of Southern France," 17 Mar. 1945, RG 407, File 107-3.5, General Archives Division, WNRC.

5. As quoted in Pogue, *George C. Marshall*, 417; Eisenhower, *Crusade in Europe*, 312; and Devers, "Operation Dragoon," 41.

6. Coakley and Leighton, *Global Logistics and Strategy*, 383–84.

7. Churchill, *Triumph and Tragedy*, 84–85.

8. Wilmot, *The Struggle for Europe*, 455, 457.

9. Ismay, *The Memoirs of Lord Ismay*, 364; and Roskill, *The War at Sea*, 3, pt. 2, 105.

10. Vigneras, *Rearming the French*, 403.

11. Coakley and Leighton, *Global Logistics and Strategy*, 370.

12. Hewitt, Transcript of Oral History, Reel 24/4, NHD.

13. Morison, *The Invasion of France and Germany*, 291; and Ruppenthal, *Logistical Support of the Armies*, 2: 124, 132–33.

14. Parrish, chief ed., *The Simon and Schuster Encyclopedia of World War II*, 582.

15. Ronald Lewin, for example, writes: "At no time . . . , did Churchill advocate a military penetration of the Balkans *on a major*

scale. The full records now in the hands of historians have destroyed this wartime (and postwar) figment, largely the by-product of American fears" (*Churchill as War Lord*, 195).

Bibliography

ARCHIVAL MATERIALS

United States National Archives, Washington, D.C. (NA)

Office of Strategic Services. *War Report*. Vol. 2.
RG 218: Joint Chiefs of Staff and Leahy File.
RG 319: Plans and Operations Division and "ABC" Decimal File.
RG 331: Sixth Army Group and Supreme Headquarters Allied
Expeditionary Force.

Foreign Military Studies (FMS)

A868: Generaloberst Johannes Blaskowitz.
A869: Major Herbert Buechs.
A875: Generalleutnant Werner Richter.
A880: Generalleutant Wend von Wietersheim.
A881: Oberstleutnant Werner Drews.
A882: Oberst Horst Wilutzky.
A884: Generalleutnant Hans Schaefer.
A888: General der Infanterie Baptist Kniess.
A946: Generalleutnant Karl Pflaum.
A960: Generalleutnant Gustav Seiz.
B203: Generalleutnant Otto Fretter-Pico.
B213: Generalleutnant Walter Botsch.
B308: Generalleutnant Bodo Zimmermann.
B376: General der Infanterie Baptist Kniess.
B486: General der Panzertruppen Walter Krueger.
B518: Generalleutnant Walter Botsch.
B556: Konteradmiral Heinrich Ruhfus.

B558: Generalleutnant Heinz von Gyldenfeldt.
B575: Generalmajor Walter Vogel.
B787: General der Infanterie Friedrich Wiese.
B800: Generaloberst Johannes Blaskowitz.

Captured German Records Microfilmed at Alexandria, Va. (NA)

T-77, Records of Headquarters, German Armed Forces High Command.
T-78, Records of Headquarters, German Army High Command.
T–311, Records of German Field Commands: Army Groups.
T–312, Records of German Field Commands: Armies.
T–313, Records of German Field Commands: Panzer Armies.
T–315, Records of German Field Commands: Divisions.

Library of Congress, Manuscript Division, Washington, D.C. (LC)

Ira C. Eaker Papers.

Center of Military History, Washington, D.C. (CMH)

United States Army, European Theater of Operations, Office of the Theater Historian. "Invasion of Southern France."
United States Seventh Army. "Diary."

United States Naval History Division, Washington, D.C. (NHD)

AFHQ, Message File, "Dragoon."
Commander, Eighth Fleet. "War Diary."

Bibliography

Commander, United States Naval Forces, Northwest African Waters. "Naval Forces, Northwest African Waters and the Eighth Fleet," 1945.
Hewitt, H. K. "Invasion of Southern France. Report of Naval Commander, Western Task Force."
Hewitt, H. K. Transcript of Oral History.

Washington National Records Center, Suitland, Md. (WNRC)

RG 338: Records of United States Army Commands, 1942–.
RG 407: Records of the Adjutant General's Office, 1917–.

United States Army Military History Research Collection, Carlisle Barracks, Pa. (USAMHRC)

Seventh Army. "G-2 History."
3rd Infantry Division Collection. "Operations Report."
United States Army. "Ammunition and Supply Operations, European Campaign."
———. Forces in the European Theater. "Supply and Maintenance."
Headquarters, 64th Fighter Wing. "XII Tactical Air Command: Tactical Operations."
Headquarters, Twelfth Air Force. "XII Air Force Service Command in Operation Dragoon."
Theodore J. Conway Papers.
John E. Dahlquist Papers.
Reuben E. Jenkins Papers.
John W. O'Daniel Papers.

York County Historical Society, York, Pa.

Jacob L. Devers Papers.

Public Record Office, London (PRO)

ADM 199: Admiralty, War of 1939–1945, War History Cases.
CAB 79: War Cabinet, Chiefs of Staff Committee Minutes.
CAB 80: War Cabinet, Chiefs of Staff Committee Memoranda.
CAB 88: War Cabinet, Combined Chiefs of Staff Committee.
CAB 99: War Cabinet, Commonwealth and International Conferences.
DEFE 3: Ultra Documents.
PREM 3: Operational Papers, Prime Minister's Office.
WO 106: War Office, Director of Military Operations and Intelligence.
WO 204: War Office, Allied Forces Headquarters Papers.

British Museum Library, London

Sir Andrew Cunningham Papers: Correspondence, ADD 52577.

Bundesarchiv-Militärarchiv, Freiburg i. Br. (BA–MA)

N6, Nachlass Walter Model.
N54, Nachlass Wilhelm Keitel.

BOOKS

Adelman, Robert H., and George Walton. *The Champagne Campaign.* Boston: Little, Brown, 1969.
Auphan, Paul, and Jacques Mordal. *The French Navy in World War II.* Trans. by A. C. J. Sabalot. Annapolis: United States Naval Institute, 1959.
Bourderon, Roger. *Libération du Languedoc Méditerranéen.* Paris: Hachette, 1974.
Bryant, Sir Arthur. *Triumph in the West 1943–1946. Based on the*

Bibliography

Diaries and Autobiographical Notes of Field Marshal the Viscount Alanbrooke. London: William Collins, 1959.

Chandler, Alfred D., Jr., ed. *The Papers of Dwight David Eisenhower: The War Years.* Vol. 4. Baltimore: Johns Hopkins, 1970.

Churchill, Winston S. *The Second World War.* Vol. 6. *Triumph and Tragedy.* Boston: Houghton Mifflin, 1953.

Coakley, Robert W., and Richard M. Leighton. *Global Logistics and Strategy,* 1943–1945. Washington, D.C.: USGPO, 1969.

Craven, Wesley F., and James L. Cate. eds. *The Army Air Forces in World War II.* Vol. 3. *Europe: Argument to V-E Day, January 1944 to May 1945.* Chicago: University of Chicago Press, 1951.

Crosia, Commandant. *Marseille 1944, victoire française.* Paris: Editions Archat, 1954.

De Lattre de Tassigny, Jean. *The History of the First French Army.* Trans. by Malcolm Barnes. London: Allen & Unwin, 1952.

Durandet, Christian. *Les Maquis de Provence.* Paris: France-Empire, 1974.

Ehrman, John. *Grand Strategy.* Vol. 5. *August 1943–September 1944.* London: HMSO, 1956.

Eisenhower, Dwight D. *Crusade in Europe.* Garden City, N.Y.: Doubleday, 1948.

Fisher, Ernest F., Jr. *Cassino to the Alps.* Washington, D.C.: USGPO, 1977.

Foot, Michael R. D. *SOE in France.* London: HMSO, 1966.

Greenfield, Kent Roberts, ed. *Command Decisions.* Washington, D.C.: USGPO, 1960. Includes essay by Maurice Matloff, "The Anvil Decision: Crossroads of Strategy," 383–400.

Guiral, Pierre. *Libération de Marseille.* Paris: Hachette, 1974.

Harrison, Gordon A. *Cross-Channel Attack.* Washington, D.C.: USGPO, 1951.

Howard, Michael. *The Mediterranean Strategy in the Second World War.* New York: Praeger, 1968.

Higham, Robin, ed. *A Guide to the Sources of United States Military History.* Hamden, Conn.: Archon Books, 1975.

Higham, Robin, and Abigail T. Siddell, eds. *Flying Combat Aircraft of the USAAF–USAF.* Ames: Iowa State University Press, 1975.

Hubatsch, Walther, ed. *Hitlers Weisungen für die Kriegführung, 1939–1945.* Frankfurt a.M.: Bernard & Graefe, 1962.

Huston, James A. *Out of the Blue: US Army Airborne Operations in World War II.* West Lafayette, Ind.: Purdue, 1972.

Ismay, Hastings, Lord. *The Memoirs of Lord Ismay.* London: Heineman, 1960.

Jäckel, Eberhard. *Frankreich in Hitlers Europa: die deutsche Frankreichpolitik im Zweiten Weltkrieg.* Stuttgart: Deutsche Verlags-Anstalt, 1966.

Lemonnier, André Georges. *Cap sur la Provence.* Paris: France-Empire, 1954.

Leslie, Peter, *The Liberation of the Riviera.* New York: Wyndham Books, 1980.

Lewin, Ronald. *Churchill as War Lord.* New York: Stein & Day, 1973.

———. *Ultra Goes to War.* New York: McGraw-Hill, 1978.

MacDonald, Charles B. *The Last Offensive.* Washington, D.C.: USGPO, 1973.

Matloff, Maurice. *Strategic Planning for Coalition Warfare, 1943–1944.* Washington, D.C.: USGPO, 1959.

Morison, Samuel Eliot. *History of United States Naval Operations in World War II.* Vol. 11. *The Invasion of France and Germany, 1944–1945.* Boston: Little, Brown, 1957.

Mueller, Ralph, and Jerry Turk. *Report after Action: The Story of the 103d Infantry Division.* Innsbruck: Wagnerische Universitäts-Buchdrückerei, 1945.

Nelson, Guy. *Thunderbird: A History of the 45th Infantry Division.* Oklahoma City: 45th Infantry Division Association, 1970.

Pappas, George S., comp. *United States Army Unit Histories.* Carlisle Barracks, Pa.: United States Army Military History Research Collection, 1971.

Parrish, Thomas, chief editor. *The Simon and Schuster Encyclopedia of World War II.* New York: Simon and Schuster, 1978.

Paszek, Lawrence. *United States Air Force History: A Guide of Documentary Sources.* Washington, D.C.: Office of Air Force History, 1973.

Paxton, Robert O. *Vichy France: Old Guard and New Order, 1940–1944.* New York: Knopf, 1972.

Bibliography

Pearson, Michael. *Tears of Glory: The Betrayal of Vercors 1944.* London: Macmillan, 1978.

A Pictorial History of the 36th "Texas" Infantry Division. Austin: 36th Division Association, 1946.

Pogue, Forrest C. *George C. Marshall: Organizer of Victory, 1943–1945.* New York: Viking Press, 1973.

Robichon, Jacques. *The Second D-Day.* Trans. by Barbara Shuey. New York: Walker & Co., 1969.

Roskill, Sir Stephen. *The War at Sea, 1939–1945.* Vol. 3. *The Offensive.* Part 2. London: HMSO, 1960.

Ruppenthal, Roland G. *Logistical Support of the Armies.* Vol. 2. Washington, D.C.: USGPO, 1959.

Schramm, Percy E., *et al. Kriegstagebuch des Oberkommandos der Wehrmacht.* 4 vols. in 7 parts. Frankfurt a.M.: Bernard & Graefe, 1961–65.

Sommers, Richard J., comp. *United States Army Military History Research Collection.* Carlisle Barracks, Pa.: United States Army Military History Research Collection, 1972.

Staiger, Jörg. *Rückzug durchs Rhônetal: Abwehr- und Verzögerungskampf der 19. Armee in Herbst 1944.* Neckargemünd: K. Vowinckel, 1965.

Sweets, John F. *The Politics of Resistance in France, 1940–1944: A History of the Mouvements Unis de la Résistance.* DeKalb: Northern Illinois University Press, 1976.

Taggart, Donald G., ed. *History of the Third Infantry Division in World War II. Washington, D.C.: Infantry Journal Press,* 1947.

Truscott, Lucian K., Jr. *Command Missions: A Personal Story.* New York: Dutton, 1954.

United States Seventh Army. *Report of Operations in France and Germany, 1944–1945.* Vol. 1. Heidelberg: Aloys Gräf, 1946.

Vigneras, Marcel. *Rearming the French.* Washington, D.C.: USGPO, 1957.

Walker, Fred L. *From Texas to Rome: A General's Journal.* Dallas: Taylor Publishing Co., 1969.

Wilmot, Chester. *The Struggle for Europe.* New York: Harper, 1952.

Wilt, Alan F. *The Atlantic Wall: Hitler's Defenses in the West, 1941–1944.* Ames: Iowa State University Press, 1975.

BIBLIOGRAPHY

THESIS

Dzwonchyk, Wayne N. "General Jacob L. Devers and the First French Army." Master's thesis, University of Delaware, 1975.

ARTICLES

Bouladou, Georges. "Les Maquis du Languedoc dans la libération," *Revue d'histoire de la deuxième guerre mondiale* 14 (July 1964): 55–80.

Devers, Jacob L. "Operation Dragoon: The Invasion of Southern France." *Military Affairs* 10 (Summer 1946): 3–41.

Guillon, Jean Marie. "Les Movements du collaboration dans le Var." *Revue d'histoire de la deuxième guerre mondiale* 29 (Jan. 1979): 91–110.

Hewitt, H. Kent. "Executing Operation Anvil-Dragoon." *United States Naval Institute Proceedings* 75 (Aug. 1954): 897–927.

———. "Planning Operation Anvil-Dragoon." *United States Naval Institute Proceedings* 75 (July 1954): 731–45.

Jenkins, Reuben E. "Operation 'Dragoon'—Planning and Landing Phase." *Military Review* 26 (Aug. 1946): 3–9.

Kahn, David. "The Ultra Conference," *Cryptologia* 3 (Jan. 1979): 1–8.

Maigne, Jean. "Les Forces françaises et la jonction 'Overlord-Dragoon.'" *Revue d'histoire de la deuxième guerre mondiale* 5 (July 1955): 17–33.

Meirat, Jean. "Dans les coulisses d'une operation combinée: le debarquement des Alliés en Provence (août 1944)." *Revue maritime* (July 1947): 102–20.

Montfort, M. "Les Combats entre Montélimar et Valence du 21 au 30 août 1944: une division blindée [11th Panzer] dans le combat et en retraite." *Revue militaire suisse.* 111 (1966): 203–63.

Sixsmith, E. J. G. "Rome, Anvil, and the Ljubljana Gap." *Army Quarterly* 99 (Oct. 1969): 52–59.

Von Donat, R. "Logistische Probleme beim Rückzug aus

Südfrankreich, August/September 1944." *Truppenpraxis* (1963): 946–51: (1964); 27–31.

RELATED WORKS

Gallico, Paul. *The Zoo Gang.* New York: Coward, McCann & Geoghegan, 1971. A group of former French Resistance fighters do good deeds in a postwar setting.

United States Army Signal Corps. "Landings in Southern France, 1944." TV-220, USAMHRC. A thirty-minute movie.

Wylie, Laurence. *Village in the Vaucluse.* 3rd ed. Cambridge: Harvard University Press, 1974. Pioneering sociological study of Peyrane, a southern French village, in the 1950s and later.

Index

Index

Jura Alps, 151

King, Ernest J., Adm., 18, 48–49
Kiska Island, 70
Kluge, Günther von, Field Marshal, 42, 43, 45, 76
Kniess, Baptist, Gen., 148
Kursk offensive, 4

La Ciotat: diversionary attack at, 112
La Coucourde, 138, 140–41
La Londe, 110, 119
Lang, Will, 83
Larche, 147, 157; Resistance activities at, 109
Larkin, Thomas, Gen., 158
Larminat, General, 125
La Rochelle, 114
La Valette, 125
Leahy, William D., Adm., 18
Le Camp, 125, 128
Le Clerc, General, 154
Leighton, Richard: assesses Dragoon, 164
Le Luc, 82, 109, 110
Lemonnier, André, Adm., 109
Le Muy, 70, 90–91, 103, 106, 111
Le Nabec, Paul, Lt. Col., 29
Levant Island, 70, 89, 143
Lewin, Ronald, 189 n
Lewis, Spencer S., Rear Adm., 101–2
Liddell Hart, Sir Basil, Capt.: evaluates de Lattre, 51–52
Life magazine, 83
Lila, Operation, 29–30
Limoges: Resistance activities near, 74
Linarès Group, 124, 125
Lincoln, George A., Brig. Gen., 46
Livron, 136, 142, 145
Ljubljana Gap, 58, 169
Lodge, Henry Cabot, Jr., Sen., 67
Loire River, 76, 169
Lons-le-Saunier, 153
Loriol, 133, 136, 140, 142
Lorraine: French battleship, 126, 145
Luftwaffe. *See* Air Force, German
Lure: capture of, 156
Luxeuil: capture of, 156
Lyons, 13, 24, 34, 65, 133, 147, 151, 154, 159; bombing attack on, 72, 73; capture of, 148–49, 150, 157; airfields near, 156; headquarters at, 157

MacDonald, Charles, 169
MacMillan, Harold, 58–59
Magnan, General, 124
Malta, 70; embarkation from, 83
Maquis. See Resistance, French
Marias, Mario R., Sgt., 106
Marignane Airfield, 79
Marines, French, 66, 70, 89–90
Marsanne Forest, 136
Marseilles, 11, 27, 28, 31, 35, 38, 55, 77, 79, 80, 82, 88, 100, 103, 108, 114, 115, 116, 118, 131, 139, 142, 144, 145, 146, 149, 159, 160, 162, 163, 168; capture of, 4, 119, 121, 124, 125, 127–31; possible invasion near, 5–6, 54; plans for capture of, 13, 24, 64; bombing attacks on, 72, 73; Resistance activities near, 74; diversion near, 92, 112
Marshall, George C., Gen., 14, 18, 19, 23, 55–56, 58, 168; assesses Dragoon, 164
Matloff, Maurice, 28, 48
Mediterranean Allied Air Forces, 14, 73, 160
Mediterranean Coastal Air Command, 83
Mediterranean theater, 2, 4, 6, 9–10, 13–14, 15, 17, 18, 20, 47–50, 55, 62, 68, 104, 145, 168
"Menado" intelligence network, 75
Meounes, 119
Meximieux, 147; capture of, 148
Military Commander, France, 31
Miramas: bombing attack on, 72
Mirkin, Victor, Maj., 126
Mistral winds, 82
Monaco, 159
Monsabert, Goislard de, Gen., 127, 128, 130, 149, 151, 163
Mont Caumes, 123, 125
Mont Cenis tunnel, 34
Mont Coudon, 123, 124–25
Montélimar, 135, 144–45, 163; capture of, 136–42; airfield near, 150
Mont Faron, 123, 125
Montfaucon, 153
Montgomery, Sir Bernard, Gen., 16
Montpellier: bombing attack on, 72
Monts des Maures, 81, 106
Mont Ventoux, 134
Mordal, Jacques. *See* Cras, Hervé
Morgan, Sir Frederick, Lt. Gen., 7, 16